66- 20743 (5-8-68)

After Victory

ALSO BY WILLIAM L. NEUMANN

America Encounters Japan: From Perry to MacArthur

AFTER VICTORY

Churchill, Roosevelt, Stalin
and the Making of the Peace

BY WILLIAM L. NEUMANN

Harper & Row, Publishers, New York, Evanston, and London

To Norman R. Morrison, 1933–1965,
who understood that peace required sacrifice

Contents

Contents

Preface

This is the history of an effort at creating a lasting peace. It was an effort which seems to have failed. The explanation is not an exploration of demonology. The peacemakers were fallible men, working to achieve their best—as they saw it—within the framework of their particular national values and interests. Churchill, Roosevelt and Stalin sought, with limited powers, to shape the future. They chose ways which they believed would best serve their nation and which would also create the kind of a world which they thought would serve the interests of mankind.

The failure of the Big Three to achieve their ends is viewed here less as an indictment of their personal qualities, flawed though they were, than as the product of the international and national systems with which they worked. It was common in World War II to condemn the old order for permitting wars to erupt. But this order was approved by the bulk of the population of Europe and the United States, who could envision no other way of organizing mankind. As leaders of open societies, Churchill and Roosevelt can be charged with doing too little to produce a flexibility of public opinion which would permit substantial changes in the international state system. Stalin can be indicted for being bound, despite his ideological affiliations, to traditional concepts in his quest for national security. But essentially the task the Big Three attempted was untying "a terrible knot, almost beyond the ingenuity of man to untie." The words are Herbert Butterfield's in his brilliant statement of the human predicament which often brings the endeavors of the best of men to tragic failure.

All historical writing involves exclusion. This history in the interests of brevity and clarity excludes many details of wartime diplomacy. Minor issues are touched on lightly or omitted altogether. The military effort is only described when it is directly relevant to the peacemakers' task. The reader in quest of more complexity and further details is referred to some of the more lengthy histories suggested in the bibliographical essay.

My thanks goes to my colleagues Rhoda Dorsey and Kenneth Walker for their critical comments on some of my chapters. I am also indebted to all those academic committee chairmen and committee members who have tolerated my less than adequate contributions while this history was in the writing.

—WILLIAM L. NEUMANN

Goucher College
Baltimore, Maryland
November 1966

1

The Persistent Task

Peacemaking, like warmaking, is a perennial activity of civilized man. The nature of the forces or interests that move men to fight their fellows en masse is still a matter of limited knowledge and differing opinions. Wars are blamed on human nature and on society. For some the villain is found in deeply rooted aggressive instincts; for others it is to be located in man-created political, economic, and social systems. Whatever the sources of man's collective belligerency, they are countered by others that produce a continuing quest for peace and the elimination of mass killings. The preambles of treaties ending wars customarily attach such adjectives as "stable," "durable," "inviolable" and, not infrequently, "perpetual" to the word "peace." While some men have devoted their dreams and energies to the creation of new weapons, others have tried to create relationships of men and nations that would eliminate international conflicts.

The instruments of war have reached almost limitless capacities for destruction. Nuclear-armed nations can now exterminate a major portion of the world's inhabitants and leave the survivors a hostile environment that may make human existence impossible. Full-scale war between such major nations thus becomes a political and moral absurdity. No civilized society, no system of govern-

1

ment, no ideological movement would draw benefits from its results.

Science and technology have brought mankind to this abyss while contributing little to the total of human wisdom on which man can draw for advice in avoiding a terminal holocaust. The newer sciences of human behavior may in time produce axioms that will guide the policymaker and the informed public on the path to a lasting peace. Mounds of data on human behavior still await a processing and analysis that may enable men to predict results of actions with a high enough degree of probability to convince the political leader and the electorate. Until that day arrives, men must rely on personal and past experience (as recorded and interpreted) as the only basis, and a crude one, for estimating the future results of present actions.

Written history is unfortunately a fallible guide. The past offers a vast warehouse of materials where each seeker with patience can find that which gives support to his convictions. The devil can quote history as well as Scripture. Statesmen in making war or peace have always been able to find historical parallels to justify their claim to being right and choosing the best policies. The list of generalizations that history "proves," according to the proponent, is almost without end.

Despite these qualifications, intelligent men can still call for the "two cheers" for history that E. M. Forster offered for democracy. Statesmen who view the present without perspective are plunging wildly into darkness in trying to prepare for the future. The past is to some extent a prologue that must be consulted. The history of nations, when analyzed with the degree of objectivity and intelligence of which men are capable at their best, is a valuable guide. Change is still neither so rapid nor so extensive as to eliminate all the continuities that warn of the limits within which man can shape the future. Men can and do make history, but they never make it in a vacuum.

When Winston Churchill, Franklin Roosevelt, and Joseph Stalin first met in 1943 to plan the creation of a peaceful world, they were taking up a task that had engaged wartime leaders since the inception of the modern state more than three centuries earlier. By conferences and congresses, by direct encounters and through mediators, kings, and emperors, political leaders and diplomats have in war sought peace. The word has been proclaimed as the objective of the most successful of generals and the most ruthless of expansionist rulers. No nation has disclaimed peace as a goal of its foreign policy.

The concept of peace (meaning only an absence of war) has never been the only objective of national policies. It is the conditions of the peace, the advantages and disadvantages to each state of the new *status quo* over which the peacemakers dispute. The men who write and sign the documents establishing the new international relationships are never principals, free to act in terms of abstract justice. They are always agents of political societies with interests to be defended and aspirations to be achieved. The constituencies of the peacemakers see the world through the distorting prisms of their own nationalism, making demands that often disregard realities and whatever codes of international equity men have created. While the best diplomats are likely to be those who can rise above their own nationalism, also understanding the distortions of others, the peace negotiators are rarely all of that caliber.

The increase of democratic participation in government and the deference national leaders must pay to an extensive public opinion have intensified the problem of the peacemaker. President Roosevelt on a number of occasions pointed out to Stalin and Churchill that he could not ignore the biases of Congress and ethnic voting blocs, regardless of the basic merits of a contrary decision. Churchill too had to adjust his decisions to his war cabinet and parliamentary coalition while even Stalin spoke of the limits of his own power to make concessions. Modern war, demanding a greater involvement and measure of sacrifice on the home front, adds to the demands of the public and intensifies the need for satisfaction. Thus the Big Three, like their long line of predecessors, sought a world of peace, but one that offered more to their peoples than a mere return to the *status quo ante bellum*.

The modern peacemaker has also had another restraint on his actions unknown to most of his counterparts in the long line of centuries of other civilizations. For the first five or six thousand years of organized warfare, ethical or moral considerations played no major part in the settlements. Decisions as to the terms of the peace were made by the victors alone when total defeat was inflicted upon the enemy. The future of the defeated political unit and its peoples was of little concern. The faiths of the ancient world often encouraged the extermination or enslavement of the population of the routed kingdom. Territories were absorbed or divided without regard for concepts of justice that might restrain the victor's desires. The praise accorded an ancient Egyptian king expressed a common attitude:

> Exulting is he, a smasher of foreheads so that none can stand near him. . . . He fights without end, he spares not and there is nothing left over.

The example of Carthage was the pattern of peacemaking long before the second-century-B.C. Roman, Porcius Cato, began his incessant demands that "Carthage must be destroyed." In the final victory, Rome acted on Cato's appeal. Carthage was leveled, its political existence ended, and the surviving Carthaginians sold into slavery. Carthage fought no more wars with Rome. Virtual extermination of the defeated polity was an effective method of maintaining peace when the victor's power was equal to the task.

The rise of Christianity introduced an ethic that in medieval Europe tempered the concept of total war and total victory. When dealing with the Moslem unbelievers of the East, however, the restraints of Christian mercy had no place. And when Christians turned on Christians in the religious wars of the sixteenth century, vengeance was unrestrained. In these struggles, in the words of J. A. Froude, "religion made humanity a crime." The peacemakers were ready to go to almost any extreme to exterminate the antichrists and to impose the true Christianity upon the defeated.

The growth of the concept of the sovereign state produced the most important change in the results of war. States now claimed a natural right to existence and to be treated even in defeat as equal in some respects to the victor. As incorporated in Hugo Grotius' great work of international law, *De jure belli et pacis* (1625), peace treaties were to be drawn according to accepted rules. Wars were to be ended by negotiations, and the victor was barred from absorbing the territory of the defeated or subjugating the enemy population. Even the conflict itself was to proceed in accordance with rules that provided for humane treatment of the wounded and the prisoners.

Grotius was never accepted completely. In the seventeenth and eighteenth centuries small German and Italian states in particular were considered fair game for conquest and absorption. More dramatically, three Christian monarchs in 1795 defied the rules in extinguishing the existence of another Christian state, Poland. But a reluctance to extinguish sovereign states became a characteristic of the victors even in the twentieth century when the methods of warfare again brought about the large-scale extermination of noncombatants. As the world became more intertwined through communication and transportation, the peacemakers continued to carry at least a minor concern for the interests and future of the defeated.

Acceptance of the concept of the sovereign state also had a direct effect on the procedural aspects of peacemaking. Beginning with the Thirty Years' War (1618–48), a formal conference of belligerents became a common European practice as a means of writing a peace treaty. If these meetings were elaborate enough they were further dignified with the name "congress." The military relationship at the time of the armistice still remained a major determinant of the settlement, but the results were the product of negotiation rather than dictation. The diplomatic skills of the contestants came into play, and the final peace was likely to express a synthesis of proposals and counterproposals. If the defeated power could produce a great negotiator, as France did in Talleyrand in 1814–15, and exploit the rivalries of the victors, the role of vengeance could be diminished further.

The arrangement of terms of peace by means of conferences produced its own procedural difficulties. National representatives demonstrated an almost unlimited sense of *amour-propre* and quarreled at length over the acts of deference that they considered proper to their status. Even though all sovereigns were theoretically equal in the eyes of God and all states equal according to natural law, for centuries the questions of precedence hindered negotiations.

The specifics of the disputes over the proper protocol are petty, if not ludicrous, although treated as solemn affairs of state. Whose representatives should be the first to enter the conference room? What are the seating arrangements at the negotiation table? In what order are signatures to be attached to the final agreements? These became matters of debate which delayed consideration of substantive matters. Behind this struggle for place was some of the same concern for recognition and pre-eminence that contributed to war.

Until the rise of Protestantism, the Papacy was the nominal head of Christendom and took precedence over all other Christian rulers. From this unchallenged position some Popes made efforts at establishing a ranking order that would avoid conflicts. Pope Julius II in 1504 assigned second place to the Holy Roman Emperor, third place to the King of the Romans and fourth to the King of France. The King of England found himself ranking eighth, below the royal houses of Portugal, Aragon, and Spain. Even if this ranking had been a rough approximation of the relative power of the European states at the time, it would have had little chance for acceptance in the face of royal jealousies. Another effort was made to create a ranking order on the basis of the antiquity of the royal house. The Papacy was accorded primacy, the Holy Roman Emperor was second, and France third with a claim to origin in Clovis, founder of the Frankish monarchy in 481. Even if historical disputes over the validity of the founding dates had not clouded this effort, venerability had too little relationship to the existing distribution of power.

Issues of protocol threatened to create almost insuperable

obstacles at the first major peace conference which brought to an end the Thirty Years' War. Delegations representing more than one hundred and thirty-five belligerents, each with a collective ego which demanded respect, faced the complicated task of arranging a settlement. The struggle for primacy between the two major victors, France and Sweden, was finally met by the device of holding two separate congresses. At Osnabruck in northwestern Germany, the Swedes and their Protestant German allies conferred with the representatives of the Holy Roman Empire. Thirty miles away in Münster, the French diplomats also met with the agents of the Holy Roman Emperor. After the date was set for the opening meetings, there was a delay of two years while the envoys wrangled over protocol. When all agreed to meet in the two cities, six months were spent there on such issues as the order in which envoys would enter the conference room and where they would sit. When a document establishing peace was finally agreed upon, three weeks were required to reach a settlement on the order in which signatures would be attached to the treaty.

The principle of absolute equality of all crowned heads and their envoys was easier to follow when peacemaking involved only two states. In the Peace of the Pyrennees in 1659, the French and Spanish diplomats met on the basis of almost perfect equality. The encounter took place on a small island in the middle of a river that marked the border between France and Spain. Identical buildings were constructed to house each delegation and a conference center built halfway between. Two doors were cut in this central structure, one facing France, the other Spain. The two delegations then entered simultaneously from their quarters and sat opposite each other in identical arm chairs.

When four powers were to meet at Ryswick in 1696, a more complicated approach was necessary to assure due respect for equality. France, England, Spain, and Holland were the principal powers. Since there was no common border, the parties settled for a small town in the Netherlands where they occupied a large villa with a central hall and two wings. Each wing was accessible by its own bridge and gate and was assigned to one set of belligerents, while the Swedish mediator was permitted to enter the central hall through the main gate. The preliminary debates included the question of the number of carriages each delegation was allowed and the number of lackeys each delegate could have in attendance. When the delegations finally agreed on how to enter the central hall, the order of seating became an issue. It was met by dispensing with a rectangular table and seating the principals in a circle. Other problems remained. Thomas Babington Macaulay described the difficulties the British and Austrian envoys had in avoiding signs of deference in approaching each other.

> The chief business of Harley and Kaunitz was to watch each other's legs. Neither of them thought it consistent with the dignity of the Crown which he served to advance towards the other faster than the other advanced towards him. If, therefore, one of them perceived that he had inadvertently stepped forward too quickly, he went back to the door and the stately minuet began again.

In the eighteenth century, rationality led to some progress on the seating problem. At Utrecht in 1713 and at Aix-la-Chapelle in 1784, the principle of *pêle-mêle* was used; delegations took seats at a circular table in their order of entry without regard to rank. But some contentious individuals continued to raise protocol issues by claiming that the place of honor was opposite the principal door and that subordinate rankings moved around the circle from the right and left.

Such questions were not allowed to block or even delay settlements when the urgency and desire for peace was great enough. When progress seemed hopelessly stalled at Ryswick, French and British representatives who were personal friends met in the privacy of an orchard and settled in two hours issues that had delayed action for two months. At Vienna in 1814–15, the complications of protocol were in large part circumvented by seeing that the Congress never met in plenary session. The important decisions were made by the envoys of the five major powers in private. At Bucharest in 1913 the same procedure was followed, but formal sessions were called to confirm private accomplishments for the sake of an interested public. In the twentieth century this became a common device for maintaining the appearance of transacting business in open sessions.

In time, procedures were established for avoiding some of the difficulties raised by the issue of precedence in a world of rapidly changing status. At Vienna in 1814, at the suggestion of Tsar Alexander, precedence at social affairs was accorded on the basis of the age of the monarchs. This gave first ranking to the King of Württemberg while the Emperor of Austria as host ranked fourth. The Tsar of Russia came after the kings of two minor states, Bavaria and Denmark. More importantly, a commission was created at Vienna to provide a permanent guide for precedence at diplomatic gatherings. Initially the commission tried to group powers in three classes, but such a distinction proved invidious and was discarded. Instead the *règlement* was drawn up that has proved its usefulness even in the twentieth century. Ranking in each national capital was established on the basis of seniority, using the date the envoy arrived at his post. Thus the doyen of the diplomatic corps is the representative longest in residence, and seating arrangements at official dinners or ranking at formal gatherings are made accordingly, with the latest arrival at the post ranking last. The United Nations rejected this system and replaced it with a lottery. Each year the Secretary General draws a name out of the list of all members; that country's ambassador comes first in precedence. Other countries are then ranked and seated in alphabetical order, beginning with the name of the country drawn first in the lottery. Attempts were also made to use a lottery to establish the order of signing treaties, but agreement was reached in 1818 at Aix-la-Chapelle to sign in alphabetical order, using the French form of the state's designation. National vanity was satisfied subsequently by the use of the *alternat*, whereby each state submits for ratification a duplicate copy of the treaty in which its own signature comes first.

While many of the older difficulties in regard to protocol have thus been eliminated, the concern for status has not disappeared. At Panmunjom in Korea in 1953, two truce teams began an endurance contest in which protocol still plays its part. The delegations meet in a hut located on the dividing line between the two Koreas with the boundary running precisely down the center of the table between the two delegations. For awhile a crease in a green felt tablecloth further established the line; but since the crease wrinkled unpredictably in favor of one side or the other, it was agreed to iron it out. Ten negotiators representing the government of North Korea and the Chinese People's Volunteers are seated on the north side of the table, with ten representatives of the United Nations Command, headed by an American, on the south. Unable to reach agreement on how to move from an armistice to a peace treaty, the delegations have emulated some of their historical predecessors in waging petty disputes. The subject matter has included the height of the chairs permitted on each side of the table and the height of the flagstaffs permitted in the room. When successive raising of the height of the flags on each side brought the flagstaffs to the roof, an agreement was reached on a reasonable height for all. The substantive business assigned by the 1953 armistice, "the unification of Korea by peaceful means under a democratic government," has been stalemated for more than a decade.

The problems of precedence and protocol have not been at the core of the peacemakers' difficulties. Generally they were matters of secondary importance, capable of dissolution by impartial formulas such as that produced by Vienna. Forms of compromise have been found in which all parties conceded little. Deviousness has sometimes eliminated the need for compromises altogether. It has been the substantive matters rather than procedural matters that have resisted solution by any *règlement* and that make the peacemaking process a difficult one.

Boundaries, control of strategic areas, and, in a variety of guises, spheres of influence have persistently been the most difficult desiderata of the peace conferences. In some geographic areas these issues long resisted permanent settlement whether approached by the Machiavellian realists or with a measure of idealism. Failure to eliminate them permanently is a characteristic of the modern international system of sovereign states.

Peace settlements consist in part of apportioning gains and levying losses and in this respect roughly reflect the military power of the participants. If the new arrangements carry too many benefits for the stronger, the grievances of the weaker are likely to produce new combinations of nations in quest of redress. And if the strong do not receive what they consider to be their just due, the *status quo* is also likely to be overturned. Even when the redrawn map reflects the distribution of power as seen by all participants, permanence is not assured. The shifting currents of strength repeatedly place existing borders and spheres of influence in jeopardy. Nations in the process of rapid growth of power seldom find the *status quo* as favorable to their interests as their rulers believe the country deserves.

Growth and decay have thus been enemies of the political *status quo* and consequently of the peace. Declining empires like those of Spain, Austria, and Ottoman Turkey invited military competition among rising powers to determine their legatees. Areas like Germany and Italy, awakened at last to a sense of common nationality, created strength where before there had been division and weakness. European history offers few examples like Swedish acceptance of Norwegian independence in 1905, when important political changes of the *status quo* were accomplished without war. Only in limited geographic areas has the work of the treaty and map maker acquired a modicum of permanence. Britain's hold on Gibraltar, acquired by treaty in 1713 and surviving more than two and a half centuries despite periodic Spanish displeasure, represents one of the exceptions rather than the rule.

The history of Russia has been an example of the periodic disturbance of the peace produced by national growth. Beginning with the reign of Peter the Great (1689–1725), this state developed the energies and strength that were periodically to upset the old order. A Europe that decried the arrival of the victorious troops of the Soviet Union in Berlin in 1945 had earlier been shocked by the Russian entry into the Prussian capital in 1761 in the course of the Seven Years' War. Even more novel than the eighteenth-century excursion westward was the triumphant parade of Russian soldiers in Paris in 1814 as part of the coalition which overthrew Napoleon.

With a population that soon exceeded that of any other major European state, the unsettling effect of Russian power and influence was periodically felt in Eastern Europe as well as southward on the shrinking borders of the Ottoman Empire. It was not until 1919, when the Bolshevik Revolution left the land of the Tsars weakened by civil war and exhaustion, that the peacemakers of Western Europe were able at Paris to push Russian boundaries eastward. Reversing the movement of more than a century, they created a Russian frontier that approximated that of 1772, before the first partition of Poland. But between 1700 and 1919 Russia was involved in twenty wars with its European and Ottoman neighbors.

A Germany unified under the leadership of Prussia has supplied another disturber of the peace. Denmark's Foreign Minister Johann Bernstorff saw the problem of the next two centuries during the Seven Years' War. He asked, in respect to Prussia, whether "a prince, having made of his states an armed camp and of his people an army, if allowed a little leisure to round out and establish his power, might become the arbiter of the grand affairs of Europe and the makeweight in the balance of powers?" By 1871 and after a series of wars, this goal was a reality. In 1914 and again in 1939, a Germany unified by destroying the *status quo* was too powerful to accept an order that seemed to deny this newcomer its place as "arbiter of the grand affairs of Europe."

The two major Western European powers, Britain and France, have also contributed to the turbulence of the international system. In Quincy Wright's compilation of modern wars, Britain ranks as the leading belligerent, active in thirty-three wars from 1700 to the opening of World War II. The first of the great commercial and industrial nations found peace generally to its interest, but the British did not forsake the use of force to extend or defend their interests whenever it was feasible. Similarly

France, with a total of twenty-eight wars in the same period, outranked only by Britain, played an active role in changing or trying to prevent changes in the *status quo*.

Many attempts have been made to associate the propensities of individual nations for war with particular characteristics of their culture, their political, economic, and ideological systems. These efforts have contributed to the understanding of a particular war or even to a series of wars, but they lose validity when applied over the course of several centuries. Those nations that fight the fewest wars in any century are not necessarily marked by a unique system or even by an abnormal national temperament. The Sweden and Switzerland that for more than a century and a half broke no peace were favored by geography to pose no obstacle to neighbors' ambitions while their national interests were capable of fulfillment without threat to others. How to construct a world in which all nations enjoy this fortunate status has been the persistent dream of many peacemakers.

2

National Traditions and Ambitions

Conflict is an intrinsic part of the international system of sovereign states. The divers national interests of any two states are never in complete accord. States that interact for the most part harmoniously still find some areas in which their outlooks clash. If this were not the rule, amalgamation through federation or union would be a simple matter and the list of sovereign states would shrink rather than continue to grow.

All conflicts are not, fortunately, productive of wars. States turn to the use of force only when the interests involved appear to be vital and when the methods for the conduct and resolution of the conflict available in peacetime seem inadequate to governments concerned. War and peace are thus more often means than ends. The military historian von Clausewitz pointed to half of this generalization in his oft-quoted statement that war was "nothing more than the continuation of politics by other means." The French Premier Georges Clemenceau completed the generalization when he said that peace was "the continuation of war by other means."

The war aims of a nation are consequently seldom far removed from the goals that nation seeks in peace. Both are a product of that state's traditional concerns for survival and se-

14

curity, its economic interests, and its aspirations for prestige and status in the international world. Under some leaders and governments these national goals are formulated more ambitiously than under others. The aspirations of the few extremist nationalists found in every state become official ends, pursued by all the machinery of that government. If the *status quo* is unsatisfactory and the policies adapted to peace produce too few changes where vital interests are concerned, the probability of war is great.

The settlements of 1919 left too many frustrated nationalists throughout Europe to create a firm *status quo*. The preamble of the Versailles Treaty stated the desires of the signatories that the condition of war "should be replaced by a firm, just and durable Peace," but produced only a twenty-year breathing period, itself marked by small wars. The description applied by C. V. Wedgwood in her analysis of the Treaty of Westphalia of 1648 was also applicable to the treaties of 1919: "a rearrangement of the European map for the next war."

For Great Britain the Paris settlements failed to achieve the traditional goals of British continental policy. An island, relying heavily on its security in the control of the seas which at one point narrowed to only twenty miles of water separating the British from their continental neighbors, this nation could never close its eyes to European developments. For at least three centuries the policy makers in London generally favored a division of power that would prevent any one nation or group of nations from dominating the entire geographic area. As Sir Eyre Crowe stated in 1907, it had become "almost an historical truism to identify England's secular policy with the maintenance of this balance by throwing her weight, now in this scale, and now in that, but ever on the side opposed to political dictatorship of the strongest single state or group at a given time." A divided and balanced Europe simplified the task of preventing a powerful nation from dominating the Low Countries, which were a potential base for launching an invasion of Britain.

To achieve or maintain a continental balance the British sought alliances with European states whose interests were also threatened by a dominant power or powers. The coalition was then employed either in fighting a war to maintain or restore the balance, or in using the techniques of peacetime diplomacy to the same end. When Europe divided itself into roughly equal national units, Britain was able to withdraw from alliances into "splendid isolation," as it was labeled, and to devote all of its energies to the defense of British hegemony over the sea routes to empire.

Successful coalition politics required of Britain a flexibility in forming and withdrawing from alliances that early earned the state the label of "perfidious Albion." But as William Pitt warned in the late eighteenth century, "to suppose that any nation can be unalterably the enemy of another is weak and childish." A nineteenth-century foreign minister, Henry Palmerston, stated the same principle bluntly when he proclaimed that Britain had "no eternal friends, nor enemies, only eternal interests." As a result, when Britain entered World War I in 1914 every major European power had been both a British ally and enemy in the course of the previous century.

At Paris in 1919, in accordance with British and French interests, a defeated Germany was barred from any future attempt to take Belgium and Holland. Articles 42 and 43 of the Treaty banned German fortifications from the banks of the Rhine and stipulated that German military forces were never to be maintained either temporarily or permanently in German territory on the left bank of the Rhine. But in 1939 the British faced a Germany, even stronger than in 1914, which had with impunity violated the Versailles settlement and remilitarized the Rhineland.

France, Britain's major ally in 1939, also found the Versailles peace inadequate. After a crushing defeat by Prussia in 1871, the French gave to Germany the place the English long held as the major enemy. When the Germans almost repeated this feat in 1914, French governments became obsessedly preoccupied with considerations of national security. "We wanted centuries of security, to be able to go on in security to the end of the world and to the Last Judgement," as Jean Giraudoux wrote in 1939.

The traditional French reliance on the greatness of the French Army and the glorious achievements under Louis XIV and Napoleon no longer promised adequate security. Losses in World War I had mounted to over 18 percent of the Frenchmen of military age compared to 15 percent for Germany and under 8 percent for Britain. Population growth had also slowed down in the 1920's far below that of Germany. Frenchmen were frequently reminded that for every three potential soldiers, the Germans had seven in the same age group, twenty to thirty. By sheer numbers a revived Germany was capable of destroying French power and undoing the work of Versailles.

Three policies were pursued by the French in their efforts to maintain their position as victors in the two decades between the wars. The political Left supported collective security and looked to a strong League of Nations. But the League members, as the first tests proved in the early thirties, were unwilling to commit their armed forces to enforce the *status quo* established in 1919. The French Right sought security in a policy of alliances, but allies were weak and unreliable. The British were even less prepared than they were in 1914 to build a large army to be landed on the continent to fight alongside the French. The Little Entente with Czechoslovakia, Yugoslavia, and Rumania also promised little in the way of military strength. The only major power to the east of Germany, the Soviet Union, despite its great manpower reserves, was still untested as a fighting force under its Communist rulers. The French Right was also hostile to Communism, and it was not until 1935 that a Franco-Soviet Pact was signed. But by that date fears of Germany were so strong, combined with hopes for a settlement with Berlin, that French policy called for avoiding any offence to Hitler by giving real support to the military pact with Moscow.

The French Army offered a third approach to security. Since World War I had been waged on the Western Front, for the most part, between two lines of trenches, they began digging in 1929 the longest and deepest trench in the world, the Maginot line. This fortification system eventually stretched along the eastern frontier of France from Luxembourg to Switzerland. To avoid any suggestion to neutral Belgium that they would not be defended by the armies of the Third Republic, the line was not extended to the sea. If the Germans obliged by attacking France on the best-defended frontier, the nation would remain secure behind this impassable barrier, despite enormous German armies.

France and Britain faced another threat in 1919, which was not that of armies but of ideas and the power of a political movement. The Bolshevik Revolution which had taken place in the land of their former Russian ally had created a peril to national security that some members of the ruling classes saw as great as that of an armed invader. Communism in Britain never won the support of more than a small minority, but the postwar restlessness of the working classes, shown in a record number of strikes in 1919, made it easy to overestimate the danger of revolution. Frenchmen too considered the Communists a real danger, supported by the example and tutelage of the Russians.

As Germany collapsed in November of 1918, the British Cabinet, according to Sir Henry Wilson, agreed that "Our real danger now is not the Boches, but Bolshevism." Premier Clemenceau suggested that the Allies construct "a barbed wire entanglement round Russia in order to prevent her from creating trouble outside." Poland, Clemenceau said, should be maintained "in order to dam up the Russian flood and to provide a check on Germany." This was the reasoning behind the *cordon sanitaire*, the barricade of small states formed out of Russian, German, and Austrian territory, ruled by an elite who were generally both anti-Russian and anti-Communist. This chain of nations was designed for a dual function, to check the spread of Communism westward, and also to block any future German expansion eastward. The new nations of Latvia, Estonia, Lithuania, Czechoslovakia, and resurrected Poland also fulfilled most of the demands of ethnic minorities who had long lived under imperial rule and who now sought political salvation in the principle of self-determination.

The rise of German power under Hitler in the thirties, along with the world economic depression which invited the growth of Communist parties in leading the mass of unemployed, created a dilemma for British and French policy. The annexation of Austria in 1938 and the absorption of Czechoslovakia in 1938 and 1939 threatened to restore Germany to a more powerful position than that held by the enemy of 1914. But Hitler also claimed to be the savior of Western civilization by blocking the expansion of the Slavic, Bolshevik hordes. If Hitler could be kept within reasonable limits without a war, his Germany could provide Britain and France with some security against Russian and Communist expansion. The Germans had made no open threats to retake Alsace-Lorraine and behind the Maginot line it might be safe to do business with Berlin.

The great cost and sacrifices necessary to cope with Hitler's Reich militarily and the value of a Nazi anti-Communist Germany politically produced in London and Paris a policy labeled "appeasement." While in both countries individuals of liberal and Marxist thought expressed horror over the racist and antidemocratic activities of the Nazi regime, the governments did not see these ideological considerations as being of major importance. As Foreign Minister Anthony Eden commented in 1942:

> What matters in foreign affairs is not the form of the internal government of any nation, but its international behavior. The trouble with Hitler was not that he was a Nazi at home. The trouble with him was that he would not stay home.

Until the spring of 1939 the British and French governments held to the hope that Hitler could be persuaded to stay home or at least limit his foreign ventures to areas of limited concern in London and Paris.

The British and French leaders who supported appeasement were expressing attitudes held by a great many of their constituents. It was unfair, as was frequently done later, to indict the leaders and disregard their supporters. The majority of Britishers and Frenchmen probably retained the hope until the fall of 1939 that Germany's ambitions could be satisfied or checked without a war. At times a large sector of the public felt that the German dictator had gone too far. The liquidation of Czechoslovakia in

March of 1939 produced a strong swing away from appeasement. The British and French governments saw Poland as the next object of German attentions and announced, with public support, that they were prepared to lend the Poles all the support in their power if Polish independence were threatened. Similar guarantees were extended to Rumania and Greece. But if it was in the vital national interest of Britain and France to fight Germany, if necessary, in order to defend Poland, neither government took adequate steps to enable that interest to be implemented in the five months between the pledge and the outbreak of war in September of 1939.

One harsh generalization can be made about Britain and France on the opening of World War II. "Our commitments had outrun our capacity," in the words of the official British war historian, J. R. Butler. The two countries went to war to check an expansionism they felt too weak to check and to honor a pledge they saw no way of fulfilling adequately. They had refused to adjust their policies to their real strength, or to create the strength necessary to implement their policies. They failed, consequently, to achieve their direct aim, the maintenance of an independent Poland.

Neither Britain nor France had any plans to try to force their way through the Baltic and bring troops or military aid to Poland. The strength of the German submarine fleet blocked any effort at direct aid by sea, and air distances were still too great for any effective aid by this military arm. French military talks with the Poles in May of 1939 had included promises of immediate air action against Germany on the outbreak of war and a major attack on the German western frontier by the sixteenth day of the war to draw strength away from the east. When these promises were redeemable in September, air action consisted of dropping propaganda pamphlets on German soil. By the sixteenth day of the war, Polish military collapse was imminent. An Anglo-French decision had already been taken on September 12 not to waste troop strength uselessly by trying to smash through the German western defense line. Anglo-French forces were more than double the German forces facing France in the first weeks of the Polish war, but the likelihood of an effective breakthrough was considered too slim and the cost in lives of any major effort too great. Polish independence was extinguished while the Warsaw radio continued to plead for aid from its allies.

If British and French goals were too ambitious for the strength they were able to organize, the same can be said for the definition given to German national interest by Hitler. Although the biographers of the Nazi leader can make claims for his historical uniqueness, the goals of Hitler's foreign policy were basically German. Most of them had been voiced by extreme nationalists before the National Socialist regime came to power in 1933. Hitler's program from the day he took office as Chancellor was directed at undoing the political setbacks of Versailles and restoring Germany to a dominant role in Europe. This was an ambitious dream held by many Germans who rejected the extreme racism and fanaticism of the Nazi domestic program.

The German outlook was closely related to the experiences that geography had brought these Central European people. Long known as the cockpit of Europe because of the many wars fought across its soil, Germany had been a victim of the rivalries of major powers without a strong central state to raise resistance. Beginning with the rise of Prussia, a new Germany was formed between the older and once more powerful states. As the new state came into existence and developed a concept of its destiny, it was easy for nationalists leaders to look about and preach the dangers of "encirclement." Germany, as they saw it, was squeezed between France on the west and Russia on the east, and barred from access to the open sea from the Baltic or Atlantic ports by British domination of the seas.

German leaders entered World War I optimistic about victory with the memories of Prussian successes in 1864, 1866, and 1871. When the first gains of 1914 seemed to confirm this optimism, a return to the *status quo ante bellum* was rejected by most political parties. A minority within the Social Democrats opposed expansionist aims, but the wartime premiers and the Reichstag generally favored redrawing the European map to give Germany not only

greater security but a strong *Mitteleuropa,* a vague concept that
meant hegemony over most of the continent.

In the course of the war, German Army spokesmen claimed
that it was essential for future security that Belgium be politically
and economically dependent on Germany. Naval expansionists
spoke of going further and annexing sections of the Belgian and
French coast to guarantee effective naval strength on the English
Channel. Both the Army and Navy spoke of this expansion as
blocking any future British troop movement to the Continent.
Industrial and business interests in Imperial Germany called for
the annexation of the French iron ore basins of Longwy-Briey,
south of Luxembourg, to assure ore in the future for the German
steel industry.

Land-hungry German expansionists also looked eastward,
coveting agricultural soils on which to feed future population. The
Treaty of Brest-Litovsk, made with a defeated Russia in March of
1918, brought substantial annexations, later taken from Germany
and assigned to the new states of Latvia and Lithuania. A reconsti-
tuted Poland was to be a German satellite, acting as a buffer
against possible Russian resurgence, while the Ukraine was to be
an independent state under German influence. Overseas annexations also appealed to some expansionists. Kaiser Wilhelm II at
one time expressed an interest in Malta, the Azores, Madeira, and
the Cape Verde Islands. Others claimed that it was in the national
interest to extend German Southwest Africa to include the Belgian
Congo and thus form a large Central African German empire.

The defeat of 1918 not only frustrated these ambitions, but
severed Germany from its colonial acquisitions as well as constricting the continental boundaries on the east and west. German
nationalists were faced with the difficult task of adjusting their
view of the national role to a smaller fatherland or of harboring
dreams and plans for the overthrow of the *status quo* created at
Paris in 1919.

By the summer of 1939 Adolf Hitler had led the nation to
the fulfillment of part of the expansionist version of national
interest. The invasion and annexation of Austria in March of 1938

gave Germany a common frontier with Italy, Yugoslavia, and Hungary and placed the German Army on the threshold of the Balkans. The Munich agreement, followed by the disintegration of Czechoslovakia in March of 1939, made Bohemia, Moravia, and Slovakia protectorates of the Third Reich. The war on Poland, preceded by a settlement with the Soviet Union on a new frontier east of Warsaw, finally brought Hitler's Germany to the possession of more territory than Germany held in 1914.

With these military triumphs Hitler became more specific in his outline of the map of the new Europe. After the fall of France in June of 1940, it was announced that Alsace-Lorraine, Luxembourg, and Norway were to be annexed to the Third Reich. A satellite state of Flemish-speaking peoples was proposed for part of Belgium while another satellite state was planned for French Brittany. With the first gains against the Soviet Union in the fall of 1941 the old plans for an independent Ukraine again were brought into the open.

The extent of these successes carried Hitler beyond the dreams of his predecessors. He envisioned the annexation of a segment of Russia that would be dominated by Germans dwelling along the Volga River and including the Caspian seaport of Baku. On some occasions the *Führer* also spoke of the desirability of making Denmark a German province and of absorbing all of the Baltic states into the new Reich. The "New Order" would have eliminated any strong rival in Europe. On the periphery Britain might remain an imperial power, but the British, like the Russians, were no longer to be permitted to play an important role on the Continent.

Hitler's ally in Rome, Benito Mussolini, also developed to the most ambitious extent the aspirations of the Italian expansionists. Like the Germans late in achieving unification, the Italians were not long in formulating a set of national interests in which security and prestige called for a number of territorial acquisitions. Deserting the Triple Alliance to enter World War I on the side of the victors, the Italians still left Paris in 1919 dissatisfied with their minor gains.

The development of the Fascist ideology and Mussolini's acquisition of power in 1923 supported a nationalist fervor that produced a grandiose vision of the national destiny. Looking to the ancient Roman past, Italians called for the recovery of their old inheritance by the establishment of a Mediterranean and African empire. "Our sea," as the Italians saw it, was a prison rather than a pathway to greatness, guarded by the British at Gibraltar and Suez and with the Greeks, Turks, and Egyptians prepared to complete the encirclement. Italy could only be secure when Malta and Corsica were out of British and French hands and when Gibraltar was demilitarized. In North Africa the Italians acquired Tripoli by conquest in 1911. Under Mussolini Ethiopia was taken in 1935. Imperialists then wrote of the need to bind the two colonies through the Anglo-Egyptian Sudan, linking Italy directly with the Indian Ocean and by-passing Suez. Others called for the creation of a North African empire, westward from Libya, reaching the Atlantic by way of Morocco and by-passing Gibraltar. Neither route to the sea offered any practical commercial or military routes to eliminate the so-called encirclement of the Mediterranean, but this did not detract from their cartographical attractiveness. And since any African empire meant an assault on British or French holdings, the Italian aspirations produced concern in London and Paris.

The last of the major European powers, Russia, received a setback for its national interests at Versailles that was comparable to that given defeated Germany. The severance of a substantial segment from Russia's western borders was a territorial loss greater than that suffered by the Tsarist regime for centuries and undid the achievements of generations. With Peter the Great's victory over the Swedes in the early eighteenth century, the Russians acquired, in the traditional phrase, "a window on the Baltic" that was consolidated by the building of St. Petersburg, present-day Leningrad. Peter's successors worked to enlarge that seacoast, absorbing Baltic lands and, with the partitions of Poland, extending Russia's frontiers westward. By 1815 this process reached its apogee with the acquisition of Swedish Finland and the creation of the Kingdom of Poland under the Tsar, both steps sanctioned by the major European powers at the Congress of Vienna.

Russian ambitions traditionally looked southward as well to the Ottoman Empire with its control of Constantinople and the Straits, constricting access to the Mediterranean. Peter the Great first pushed Russian power to the Black Sea by war against the decadent but resilient Ottomans. Successive Russian rulers broadened control of the Black Sea coast and absorbed Bessarabia on the future Rumanian frontier as well as lands of the Caucasus between the Black and Caspian seas.

As Russian status as a great power became assured by the end of the eighteenth century, the ambition to control the exit of the Black Sea became greater. When Catherine the Great made a triumphal visit in 1787 to Kherson, near the mouth of the Dnieper, she rode under an arch heralded as "the way to Constantinople." The growing influence of Britain in the Sultan's affairs in the nineteenth century, culminating in the use of the Straits by British and French fleets to enter the Black Sea and invade the Crimea, greatly strengthened the arguments of Russian nationalists for the control of Constantinople as essential to national security. Promoters of ambitious concepts of Russian destiny also appealed to the old faith of the Orthodox in Moscow as the "Third Rome," with the mission of one day driving the pagans out of the center of Orthodox Christianity, and restoring Constantinople and the Holy Land to Christian rule. Toward the end of the nineteenth century the romantic appeals of Pan-Slavism contributed new support for these claims of destiny in the Balkans.

Russian fears and aspirations grew strong during World War I when Turkey, aligning itself with Germany, entered the war with an attack on Russian Black Sea ports while closing the Straits to Russian commerce and cutting a major means of communication with the Western Allies. In the course of the war, both Britain and France agreed that on the defeat of the Central Powers Constantinople and the Straits would be finally assigned to Russia. Ironically, it was the Bolshevik Revolution and the decision of the Soviet leaders to make peace with Germany that deprived Russia of presenting her claims at Paris in 1919. Britain and France both took their share of the Ottoman Empire in the form of mandates, but Constantinople was retained by the Turks and renamed Istanbul in 1930.

The Bolshevik regime under Lenin not only rejected the old political and economic order of the Tsars, but for a few years repudiated the traditional goals of Russian foreign policy as well. Although the creation of an independent Finland brought a foreign power to within twenty miles of Leningrad, the Russians were not initially concerned about this threat. In their early optimism and expectation of a revolution that would make all Europe socialist, the Bolsheviks not only accepted the claims to independence of the Finnish nationalists, but disavowed the secret treaties with the Allies that had promised territorial gains.

There was evidence in a short time that there were limits to the losses that avowed Communist internationalists would permit to be inflicted on the Russian motherland. When in 1920 the Poles under Premier Pilsudski tried to exploit Russian weakness and push eastward, hoping to create a satellite state in the Ukraine, the Bolsheviks and the Red Army fought so vigorously that at one point they pushed the Poles back to the outskirts of Warsaw. Polish victories then forced the Bolsheviks to accept a western boundary in the Treaty of Riga, which ceded more Russian territory to the new state than had been assigned Poland at Paris in 1919.

Russian foreign policy between 1920 and 1939 remained defensive while paying more respect to traditional Tsarist policies. The primary concern of the Communist state was to rebuild national strength before a new invasion came from the western states. As an outcast from the society of nations proclaimed at Paris, the Russians joined the other major outcast, Germany, and in the Treaty of Rapallo in 1922 re-established diplomatic and commercial relations. Stalin, as Lenin's successor, continued the drive to build a powerful state before the foreign aggressors once more tried to destroy the Socialist experiment. As he said in 1931:

Those who fall behind get beaten, but we do not want to get beaten. The Mongol Khans beat Old Russia. The Turkish beys beat her. The Swedish feudal lords beat her. The Polish-Lithuanian "squires" beat her. The Anglo-French capitalists beat her. The Japanese barons beat her. They all beat her for backwardness. That is why we must no longer be backward. We are fifty to a hundred years behind the advanced countries.

With a sound estimate of future developments, Stalin went on to predict, "We must make good that distance in ten years. Either we do it, or they crush us."

With the rise of a powerful and threatening Germany under Hitler, the Soviet regime was faced with the same ambivalence felt in London and Paris. The Russians distrusted the capitalist states who had sent military expeditions that intervened in the civil wars on the side of the anti-Bolshevik forces. But, other than fighting Germany alone, they had either to appease Hitler or seek western allies. When the Soviet Union was admitted to the League of Nations in 1934, Foreign Minister Maxim Litvinov became a vigorous supporter of collective security. The Soviet Union continued to express support of that principle even as the incapability of the League was demonstrated in respect to the Japanese attacks on China and the Italian attack on Ethiopia, followed by Italian intervention in the Spanish Civil War.

The Russians suffered a major rebuff from the Munich settlement, being neither invited to the four-power conference nor consulted in the fate of their Czech neighbor. When the October 1938 agreement was followed by Hitler's absorption of the rest of the Czech state, German forces moved to within striking distance of the Ukraine. As Hungary also joined the Nazi camp, the Russians were placed in a dangerous situation. Negotiations were begun in April of 1939 at Moscow with Britain, but London failed to send its first-rank negotiators, and the responses to Moscow proposals came from London with what the Russians regarded as deliberate slowness. The two states that Britain and France had guaranteed against German attack, Poland and Rumania, were unwilling to risk German displeasure and enter into arrangements for their defense with the Soviet Union even indirectly. The Poles were particularly reluctant to deal with the Russians for good historical reasons. "With the Germans we risk losing our liberty," said Marshal Smigly-Rydz; "with the Russians we risk our soul." Colonel Josef Beck, the Polish Foreign Minister, saw his country's predicament in a similar light: "If the Soviet Union is militarily feeble, what good is it to be tied to it; if the Soviet Union is strong they will never leave the Polish regions they occupy."

With the Poles in effect choosing to throw in their lot with the Germans, the British and French could do little in working out effective military co-operation with the Russians. Churchill heard the Russian side later, directly from Stalin:

> We formed the impression that the British and French Governments were not resolved to go to war if Poland were attacked, but that they hoped the diplomatic line-up of Britain, France and Russia would deter Hitler. We were sure it would not.

Stalin in 1939 also recognized that the military strength that Britain and France were willing to expend against the Germans was quite inadequate. When the Russians asked what forces the French would send against the Reich, they were given the optimistic figure of a hundred divisions while the British promised to send two at once on the outbreak of war and two later. Since Stalin believed that the Russian Front would require three hundred divisions for victory, he did not see his potential Western Allies as bearing an equitable share of the manpower burden.

Sometime in 1939, at a date still clouded with historical disputes, the Russians began simultaneous talks with the Germans which led to the Nonaggression Pact on August 23, 1939. While this pact assured Hitler of Russian neutrality while he attacked Poland, it also gave the Soviet Union a further twenty-two months to prepare for what Moscow considered would be an inevitable war with Hitler's Germany. Stalin's critics indict him for his failure to use this breathing period to build all the strength necessary, but the Soviet Union was still stronger in 1941 than in 1939. By secret agreement with Berlin, the Russians received a large slice of Polish territory, an area that served as a small buffer when the Nazi invasion finally began in June of 1941. The fall of France in June of 1940 and the flight of British forces across the Channel confirmed the Soviet estimates of the military weakness of their prospective allies. Even Churchill, looking back on the Nazi-Soviet agreement, believed that "If their policy was cold-blooded, it was also at the moment realistic in a high degree."

Before the German attack took place, the Russians expanded further in preparation for war. The small Baltic states of Latvia, Lithuania, and Estonia were pressed into signing nonaggression pacts that then led to their absorption by the Soviet Union. A war was also launched against Finland that ended in March of 1940 when the Finns agreed to cede the Karelian Isthmus, creating a substantial buffer for the exposed city of Leningrad and one that served well in enabling that city to survive the German onslaught. The Soviet view of national interest in respect to the European frontier by 1940 had come close to the traditional Tsarist policy of achieving a strong position on the Baltic and in Eastern Europe.

The aims in peace and war of another major power, Japan, also became important in World War II. The Japanese were neophytes in the play of world politics compared to their European allies and adversaries. They had been projected into the whirl of imperialist competition by the success of the American naval expedition of 1853–54, which opened Japan to the inrush of European competitors. But instead of succumbing like China and continuing to suffer the inequities of an inferior relationship with the Western powers, Japan responded with an amazing burst of westernization in industrial and military techniques. The Japanese nationalists were also quick to create and in some instances to revive ancient imperialist ambitions to expand the empire. By the end of the nineteenth century, the Ryukyu Islands and Formosa had been joined to Japan by war and occupation.

Like the major European powers, Japan's definition of its

security needs became an expanding one as the state grew in power. Korea was transformed into "a dagger aimed at the heart of Japan," a dagger that came under Japanese control and occupation after a successful war with Russia in 1904–5. In World War I further ambitions were expressed and fulfilled by acquiring the German-held islands of Micronesia, stretching into the South Pacific, and the German rights in China's Shantung Peninsula. An ominous development for the Russians was the joint Japanese-American occupation of eastern Siberia in the course of the civil wars following the Bolshevik Revolution. The Japanese were slower to evacuate this area than the Americans when the wars ended, and the Russians saw lingering ambitions in Tokyo.

A lull came in Japanese expansionism during the 1920's, but this was ended when military adventurers brought Manchuria under national control in the early thirties. The presence of Japanese troops on the Siberian border became a matter of continued concern for Moscow. When Japan joined the Rome-Berlin Axis in September of 1940, signing a ten-year military alliance, the Soviet Union had to consider the possibility of an invasion on two fronts.

Japan's national interests, as defined in the 1930's, also clashed with those of the United States. Tokyo's ambition to become the leader of the Oriental peoples and to exert a hegemony in Asia was felt to be a threat to the Philippines as well as to that vague but important set of American interests grouped under the concept of the "Open Door" in China.

The international system by 1939 was no longer one of the normal level of peacetime conflict. The national interests of the major powers, shaped by tradition and ambition, were such that the policies available in peacetime no longer promised adequate satisfaction. War, offensive or defensive, was the only policy that seemed likely to achieve the desired national ends.

3

Peace as an American Interest

Unique elements in the American experience produced a conviction that peace was always the goal of "good nations" and war the work of the "bad nations." The European thesis that war was a normal aspect of the relations of sovereign states, rather than always the product of evil men, never gained much strength in American thinking about international relations. Americans have also held the belief that, of all peace-loving nations, it was the United States that most fully exemplified this virtue. For more than a century and a half this framework of thinking dictated avoidance of any political connections with European nations because of the danger of involvement in the wars produced by the power politics and historic rivalries of the Old World.

American faith in peace has always appeared to have been demonstrated by this country's history. The conquest of the continent of North America involved few military engagements large enough to be categorized as wars, due to the weakness of the American Indian in numbers and weapons. Few Americans think of the heroic conquest of the West as a series of almost continuous acts of violence against the original occupants. The foreign wars the United States entered prior to World War II were small, brief, and involved few sacrifices. The total combat deaths of American

31

forces in the War of 1812, the Mexican War, the Spanish-American War and World War I were under 60,000, fewer than some European nations lost in one bloody campaign.

Prior to Pearl Harbor in 1941, the United States also had not had the experience of being directly subject to initial military attack. Even the Japanese bombs fell on a distant island possession. The declarations of war in 1812, in 1846, in 1898, and in 1917 were decisions reached by the President and Congress without foreign troops crossing the United States borders. Only in the Mexican War was there even a claim of an intrusion by Mexican troops, and an unconvincing claim, as Abraham Lincoln's challenge showed.

Between its wars the United States had little need of concern for military strength and managed to maintain only minimal armies and navies without paying a serious penalty. The total experience was one of "free security," as Professor C. Vann Woodward has pointed out. This left little experience with which to understand the tensions experienced by European nations that had periodically experienced armed invasions. Nor were Americans readily capable of recognizing the amoral characteristics of international relations and accepting the linking of peace and war policies pointed out by von Clausewitz. As a result the American approach has been frequently criticized for its moralism, utopianism, and false idealism in disregarding the essential characteristics of the world of sovereign states. These same qualities attributed to the outlook expressed by Americans have also produced a national repugnance for international compromises, the pragmatic settlements forged out of mutual concessions that have traditionally been the achievement of great diplomats and statesmen.

The experience of the United States in World War I seems to have fully evoked these unique attitudes. The results of that conflict, as interpreted by many American writers in the 1920's and 1930's, had one major lesson. Any future peace, to be a lasting one, had to be based on American ideals. Allies were to be committed to these broad goals as early as possible, and all question of their specific application to the complexities of reality had to be deferred until the war was over. The great mistake of

World War I seemed to have been the making of secret wartime treaties in which potential spoils were divided, rather than awaiting the peace to establish a settlement based on justice.

President Roosevelt and many members of his administration were influenced to some degree by this unsophisticated and over-simplified interpretation of Wilson's defeat at Paris. Roosevelt was himself a member of the Wilson cabinet as Assistant Secretary of the Navy. He had supported the foreign policy of the President wholeheartedly and remained a part of the administration during the months of negotiations in Paris and debates in Congress. As vice-presidential candidate in 1920, he had defended Wilson and experienced the overwhelming Democratic defeat that was attributed by many to Wilson's handling of foreign affairs. "The tragedy of Wilson was always somewhere within the rim of his consciousness," Robert Sherwood wrote of Roosevelt. When the United States entered World War II, the President was determined to avoid the errors of his Democratic predecessor.

In 1939 as in 1914 there was general confidence in Washington that this country would take no active part in the European conflict. Sympathies for Britain and France and animosity for Germany were probably stronger than they had been in 1914, but there were few calls for American involvement. Among Americans, as among Europeans, there was fear that the conflict would begin with a great carnage from air attacks on the major cities. Instead London, Paris, and Berlin were spared, and even the troops in combat received only propaganda leaflets from the air. After the fall of Poland in October of 1939, there were no major military engagements in the West, and Americans began to look with detachment on what was known as the "Phony War."

Noninvolvement militarily did not preclude official and unofficial interest in taking some part in any future peace settlement. The Roosevelt administration felt some responsibility for being better prepared to guide the peacemakers in proper channels than had been the case at Paris in 1919.

American planning for the peace in World War I had been undertaken by a commission of private scholars brought together at the suggestion of President Wilson's friend and adviser, Colonel Edward House. Sidney Mezes, son-in-law of House and president of City College of New York, was authorized late in 1917 to gather leading American experts in a group later known as "The Inquiry." Papers were commissioned on a wide range of subjects to be used in guiding future peacemakers. The first subject of a preliminary outline was "Suppressed, Oppressed, and Backward Peoples, etc." with the Poles, Bohemians, Yugoslavs, and Africans falling under this heading. Another directive called for "Data and sane proposals regarding war-breeding areas" and listed the major geopolitical issues of Europe and the colonial areas for examination.

The research was well organized, and the distinguished scholars produced many studies, some of high quality. But the task exceeded the resources of the American intellectual community. Walter Lippmann, secretary of "The Inquiry," said after six months of work that for many problems of primary importance there was "a real famine in men." Russia, the Balkans, Turkey, and Africa were listed as "lands intellectually practically unexplored," at least by Americans. For lack of specialists, an able young Harvard professor of colonial American history was set to study the problems of Finland, while a Latin-American expert was assigned to Turkey. In Eastern Europe and the Balkans, studies frequently relied on *émigré* consultants, men whose own grievances and nationalist aspirations grossly distorted the information and evaluations that they furnished.

Faulty intelligence reports from Europe also led to bad judgments as to what possibilities were going to be open at the peace. This was particularly true in respect to Russia. The Bolshevik regime was assumed to be transitory, and the Russian Empire, rent by civil war, was expected to remain fragmented. Recommendations were consequently made for the formation of an independent Ukraine. Japan was to be rewarded for participation in the war by being ceded an important sector of Siberia. The northern half of the divided island of Sakhalin and Russia's maritime provinces east of the Amur River, along with the port of

Vladivostok, it was proposed, could be sold to Japan in return for Japanese cancellation of the Tsarist regime's indebtedness to Japan. This radical proposal seems to have had as its ulterior American motive the diversion of Japanese expansionism into northern Asia, thus safeguarding the Philippines and perhaps China. No action was taken at Paris on this proposal. By the perversity of history, the United States took a major part, twenty-five years later, in turning the entire island of Sakhalin over to Russia after driving the Japanese off the Asian mainland.

It was not "The Inquiry" that had the most important influence on the peace of 1919, but the President's statement on peace aims of January 8, 1918, subsequently made famous as the Fourteen Points. In addressing Congress on that date, Wilson said that the United States demanded "that the world be made fit and safe to live in," and that unless justice was done to others, it would not be done to the United States. The only possible program for a just peace, he said, was the Fourteen Points he presented (see pages 36–37).

Wilson was pressed into producing his statement by the actions of the Bolsheviks in opening the Tsarist archives and revealing the secret treaties with the other Allied powers. In the tradition of European politics these arrangements apportioned the expected gains of victory. But they contrasted strongly with the ideals for which President Wilson said the United States was fighting. The Fourteen Points were an effort to press the future peace into the framework of his "New Diplomacy" in which traditional national interests would be discarded in favor of some abstract concepts of justice.

Wilson's program had resemblances to other statements produced by spokesmen of liberal and socialist groups in Britain and Europe. The Union for Democratic Control in Britain had proclaimed its opposition to secret diplomacy and to continued armaments when it was founded in 1914, and it worked for an acceptance of a peace to be based on the self-determination of peoples, the removal of trade barriers, and the creation of a League of Nations. In Russia the Bolsheviks had proclaimed some similar

THE FOURTEEN POINTS

I. Open covenants of peace, openly arrived at, after which there shall be no private international understandings of any kind but diplomacy shall proceed always frankly and in the public view.

II. Absolute freedom of navigation upon the seas, outside territorial waters, alike in peace and in war, except as the seas may be closed in whole or in part by international action for the enforcement of international covenants.

III. The removal, so far as possible, of all economic barriers and the establishment of an equality of trade conditions among all the nations consenting to the peace and associating themselves for its maintenance.

IV. Adequate guarantees given and taken that national armaments will be reduced to the lowest point consistent with domestic safety.

V. A free, open-minded, and absolutely impartial adjustment of all colonial claims, based upon a strict observance of the principle that in determining all such questions of sovereignty the interests of the populations concerned must have equal weight with the equitable claims of the government whose title is to be determined.

VI. The evacuation of all Russian territory and such a settlement of all questions affecting Russia as will secure the best and freest co-operation of the other nations of the world in obtaining for her an unhampered and unembarrassed opportunity for the independent determination of her own political development and national policy and assure her of a sincere welcome into the society of free nations under institutions of her own choosing; and, more than a welcome, assistance also of every kind that she may need and may herself desire. The treatment accorded Russia by her sister nations in the months to come will be the acid test of their good will, of their comprehension of her needs as distinguished from their own interests, and of their intelligent and unselfish sympathy.

VII. Belgium, the whole world will agree, must be evacuated and restored, without any attempt to limit the sovereignty which she enjoys in common with all other free nations. No other single act will serve as this will serve to restore confidence among the nations in the laws which they have themselves set and determined for the government of their relations with one another. Without this healing act the whole structure and validity of international law is forever impaired.

VIII. All French territory should be freed and the invaded portions restored, and the wrong done to France by Prussia in 1871 in the matter of Alsace-Lorraine, which has unsettled the peace of the world for nearly fifty years, should be righted, in order that peace may once more be made secure in the interest of all.

IX. A readjustment of the frontiers of Italy should be effected along clearly recognizable lines of nationality.

X. The peoples of Austria-Hungary, whose place among the nations we wish to see safeguarded and assured, should be accorded the freest opportunity of autonomous development.

XI. Rumania, Serbia, and Montenegro should be evacuated; occupied territories restored; Serbia accorded free and secure access to the sea; and the relations of the several Balkan states to one another determined by friendly counsel along historically established lines of allegiances and nationality; and international guarantees of the political and economic independence and territorial integrity of the several Balkan states should be entered into.

XII. The Turkish portions of the present Ottoman Empire should be assured a secure sovereignty, but the other nationalities which are now under Turkish rule should be assured an undoubted security of life and an absolutely unmolested opportunity of autonomous development, and the Dardanelles should be permanently opened as a free passage to the ships and commerce of all nations under international guarantees.

XIII. An independent Polish state should be erected which should include the territories inhabited by indisputably Polish populations, which should be assured a free and secure access to the sea, and whose political and economic independence and territorial integrity should be guaranteed by international covenant.

XIV. A general association of nations must be formed under specific covenants for the purpose of affording mutual guarantees of political independence and territorial integrity to great and small states alike.

In regard to these essential rectifications of wrong and assertions of right, we feel ourselves to be intimate partners of all the governments and peoples associated together against the Imperialists. We cannot be separated in interest or divided in purpose. We stand together until the end. . . .

principles shortly before Wilson's speech, going a radical step
further and holding that the right of self-determination applied
not only to Europe but to the colonial peoples of Asia, Africa, and
the Near East as well. It was Wilson's speech, however, that had
the greatest initial effect in arousing the hopes of Europe for a
permanent and just peace. The Fourteen Points lifted the morale
of liberal elements among the Allies as well as encouraging the
growing peace forces in Germany.

Wilson's aims were less successful—some would say a failure
—in shaping the Paris treaties. As a proponent of "peace without
victory," the President reluctantly signed a document that was
dictated to, rather than negotiated with, Germany. Whatever its
merits or demerits, the peace was a different sort from that which
had ended the major wars in the previous two centuries. "Gone
were the days of the Treaties of Utrecht and Vienna," wrote
Winston Churchill, for now the peoples of Europe "stood around
in scores of millions to demand that retribution should be exacted
to the full." The settlement was not a Carthaginian peace, but it
seemed to be a step in the direction of the earlier form in which
the defeated power was to be permanently eliminated as a major
state.

Many who believed in Wilson and the ideals of the Wilsonian peace felt betrayed. By 1927 Harold Lasswell could write
of "that credulous utopianism which fed upon the mighty words
which exploited the hopes of the mass in war." Now, as he saw it,
these sentiments had given way to "cynicism and disenchantment."
Roosevelt himself shared some of the disillusionment of those
years and knew that the majority of Americans came to believe that
it had been a mistake to have even entered the European war. A
national poll in November of 1939 still found twice as many
voters believing that it had been wrong to go to war in 1917 as
those who more than twenty years later still approved the action of
Wilson and the Congress.

When President Roosevelt became convinced that he must
take up Wilson's task and lead this country into another war, he
fully recognized the weight of the resistance to such action left by

the popular interpretation of the results of 1917. Events, helped by Presidential interpretations, slowly broke the old mold of thought. After the fall of France in the summer of 1940 and the unchallenged spread of German power on the continent, many Americans began to face the thought of a new war. By April of 1941 only 39 percent of the voters polled still felt that Wilson had made a mistake, compared to the 43 percent who now saw the first war against Germany as justified. Still Roosevelt had to be cautious to avoid obvious parallels that might add to the power of his domestic opponents. In the 1940 campaign he had catered directly to the isolationist sentiment with his promises that American boys would never be sent to "foreign wars."

Already in December of 1939 a committee was established within the Department of State to deal with the problems of "peace and reconstruction." The professionals of the Department had not welcomed the incursion of outsiders in the form of "The Inquiry" and proposed that all preparations for the peace be carried out within the sphere of the Secretary of State. Under Secretary of State Sumner Welles was appointed to head the new committee, but Welles and other committee members were too fully engaged in current diplomatic issues to give adequate time to studies of the future. By early 1940 the committee did explore the idea of forming an organization of neutral states, not only to strengthen their co-operation during the war years, but also to consider the role that neutrals might play in shaping the peace. President Roosevelt seemed initially favorable to such a proposal, and exploratory conversations began with some forty-seven neutrals of whom twenty were Latin-American states.

As in World War I, the neutrals had many grievances. These were directed not only against German submarine warfare but also against the British blockade of Europe and control of the high seas in disregard of traditional neutral rights. Any conference would have been sure to raise these complaints, and the United States, out of friendship to Britain and itself tolerating these maritime practices, would have been an embarrassed sponsor. President Roosevelt decided that it would be inadvisable to take the leadership in organizing the neutrals, and the proposed conference was never called. Instead the President announced on February 9, 1940, that he was sending Sumner Welles to Europe to talk with the leaders of the warring states.

The Welles mission was never officially acknowledged as an exploration of the possibilities of a negotiated peace, but this was one of its objectives along with gathering information for presidential review. The Under Secretary went twice to Rome and visited foreign secretaries and officials in Berlin, Paris, and London. The only specific American suggestions for the peace Welles brought were disarmament and the liberalization of international trade by removing barriers to the free flow of goods. His proposals were vague enough to raise no objections, and even Hitler agreed with Welles on the desirability of disarmament and freer trade in the future.

By stopping first at Rome in February of 1940, the American representative sought to encourage the nominally neutral Italians to remain so. Welles also brought Mussolini an invitation from Roosevelt to a meeting somewhere outside their two countries. After canvassing Italian views on the nature of German war aims and the possibilities of peace negotiations, Welles went on to Berlin. Both Hitler and Foreign Minister von Ribbentrop told him that Britain was committed to the overthrow of the Nazi regime and the destruction of the German state; a negotiated peace was, therefore, an impossibility. Secretly planning their spring offensive against France and optimistic about its success, the Germans were poor prospects for a peace conference.

In Paris, Welles found the French also optimistic about future military victory. The war was not popular with some segments of society, but the French government was moving to enlist their support by means of an indirect war with an even larger opponent, the Soviet Union. This was a war to be fought on Finnish and Russian soil. The Soviet attack on Finland, which began at the end of November 1939, produced urgent appeals from Helsinki to Paris and London for help with planes and munitions. The American ambassador to Paris, William Bullitt, informed Washington on January 15, 1940 that:

> The French position is that France will not break diplomatic relations with the Soviet Union or declare war on the Soviet Union, but will if possible destroy the Soviet Union—using cannon, if necessary.

This improbable-sounding dispatch referred to the fantastic plans being made to win the support of Frenchmen who thought that Hitler and Nazism were secondary dangers and that Stalin and Communism were the real enemies. A proposal was actually sent to London for the dispatch of a joint expeditionary force to Finland and for an Anglo-French naval expedition to the Black Sea. The naval force was to have as its target the Russian cities of Batum and Baku, the latter on the Caspian Sea, to be destroyed by air attacks, eliminating an important source of oil for both the Soviet Union and Germany. Since neither the French nor the British had as yet launched air attacks against German military installations, this boldness in planning to bomb Russian cities suggests the intensity of the planner's feelings against the Soviet Union. Fortunately, the British acted as a check on these schemes.

There was an interest in London in a joint invasion of Scandinavia that would not only aid the Finns but also seize the Norwegian ore fields, which were currently of great value to the German steel industry. The Supreme War Council planned this action with "an air of unreality," according to the official British military history. The earliest date the landings could be made was March 20, 1940; but by that date the Finns had made peace with the Russians, and the German invasion of Norway on April 9 caught the British still planning their own surprise.

When Welles began his talks with Prime Minister Daladier in Paris on March 7, the Russo-Finnish peace talks were beginning. Daladier still expressed a willingness to make peace with Germany on a basis that accepted some revisions of the *status quo* of early 1938. The French leader was willing to see the Sudeten-

land and the German-populated areas of Poland go to the Reich if
both the Poles and the Czechs could be assured of the political
independence of the remaining territory. The retention of Austria
was also acceptable to France if a plebiscite showed that the
Austrian people desired such a union.

The major French concern over a negotiated peace was not
the territorial adjustments, but fear that Berlin would not honor
any of its engagements, and that Hitler would not stop short of
trying to dominate all of Europe. The chief need of France and its
neighbors, according to Daladier, was for security. This, he suggested, could only be provided by a powerful neutral like the
United States acting as a guarantor of any new rearrangement of
the map of Europe. Police work to maintain the peace, Daladier
thought, could be done by an international air force.

In London, Welles encountered a range of views about the
future peace. At one extreme was the First Sea Lord, Sir Dudley
Pound, who felt that at the conclusion of the war Berlin should be
destroyed, Germany divided into several small states, and the
major German cities occupied by British and French troops for at
least fifty years. At the other extreme was the great leader of
World War I, Lloyd George, who saw no reason why Germany
should not be permitted to unite the Germanic peoples of Europe
and hold a special economic position in Central and Southeastern
Europe. Winston Churchill, not yet Prime Minister, saw no peace
without the defeat of Germany and the overthrow of the Nazi
government. Prime Minister Chamberlain was willing to talk
about the unlikely possibility of a negotiated peace with Hitler, but
said that it would require a demonstration of good faith on the
part of Berlin in the form of a preliminary evacuation of Poland,
Bohemia, and Moravia.

Chamberlain suggested that Welles extend his inquiries to
Moscow, although this capital had not been included in his itiner-
ary. Roosevelt may have been unwilling to risk the domestic
repercussions such a visit would have evoked at this time. The anti-
Russian feelings raised by Soviet occupation of eastern Poland in
September of 1939 were heightened by the attack on Finland. In

February of 1940 the House of Representatives came within three votes of eliminating all salaries and expenditures for the American embassy in Moscow in an effort to force a break in diplomatic relations with the Soviet Union. Washington's estimates of Russian military strength, based on the initial Soviet failures in the Finnish campaigns, were so low as to dismiss the Red Army as an important factor in the immediate future of Europe.

If President Roosevelt had any thought of mediating the European war, Welles' reports were discouraging. No basis of negotiations was evident between London and Berlin. Welles returned convinced of one matter, that security in Europe, aided by some measure of disarmament, was more important for the future peace than any of the territorial or economic issues. If the United States could propose a practical plan for security that would convince Europe of its effectiveness, a lasting peace was possible.

Any consideration in Washington of a new security system was almost immediately diverted by the drama of military events. The German sweep into Norway and Denmark, beginning on April 9, was followed in May by a victorious swing through Holland and Belgium and the fall of France in June. The resulting German dominance of Western Europe was disturbing. Roosevelt, who decided at this time to run for an unprecedented third term, began a series of emergency measures to prevent the collapse of Great Britain. As the United States moved from nominal neutrality to semi-belligerency, the President spoke of the need of avoiding "a dictator's peace."

With the United States moving closer to entry into the European war, the President recognized the value of encouraging high morale by speaking of the ideals that he believed were, or should be, involved in this struggle. Several times in 1940 he spoke of the kinds of freedom upon which a peaceful world must be based and contrasted these ideals with the proclamations of the Nazi regime. In his annual message to Congress in January of 1941, Roosevelt requested the passage of the Lend-Lease Bill to expand aid to Britain. In the same message the President enunciated what came to be known as the Four Freedoms:

THE FOUR FREEDOMS

The first is freedom of speech and expression—everywhere in the world.

The second is freedom of every person to worship God in his own way—everywhere in the world.

The third is freedom from want—which, translated into world terms, means economic understandings which will secure to every nation a healthy peacetime life for its inhabitants—everywhere in the world.

The fourth is freedom from fear—which, translated into world terms, means a world-wide reduction of armaments to such a point and in such a thorough fashion that no nation will be in a position to commit an act of physical aggression against any neighbor—anywhere in the world.

These ideals were even more utopian in character and geographic scope than Woodrow Wilson's statements. Doubts were expressed that the President really believed, as he said, that these freedoms were "attainable in our time and generation." Harry Hopkins, as intimate with Roosevelt as any of his aides, assured Robert Sherwood that these were not catch phrases: *"He believes them."* Hopkins had asked Roosevelt when the speech was being drafted whether he wanted to include that sweeping phrase, "everywhere in the world," and reminded him that this included "an awful lot of territory." Hopkins said that it might not produce a favorable political response in Americans who were not interested in exotic places like Java. Roosevelt's answer was that the world was too small for Americans to ignore even the Javanese, who were now neighbors.

In the same address the President attacked the prevailing critical view of the 1919 peace. "We need not overemphasize imperfections in the Peace of Versailles," he said, since it was far less unjust than the kind of pacification that Hitler was inflicting upon Europe.

In August of 1941 the major statement of Anglo-American idealism was presented to the world by Roosevelt and Churchill at the Atlantic Conference. The President could not shake the fear that he would be confronted, like Wilson, with some secret wartime agreements that would conflict with the American concept of the peace. With the entry of the Soviet Union into the war, following the German attack on June 22, 1941, there was a possibility that London and Moscow might reach some agreement about Eastern Europe. To prevent this, Britain was to be united with the United States in a statement of peace aims.

Roosevelt looked forward to the Atlantic Conference as an opportunity to talk directly with Churchill. The two men had corresponded confidentially from September of 1939 and felt a mutual affinity, based in part upon their interest in naval affairs and service during World War I. A naval rendezvous was arranged with great secrecy for the ninth of August in Argentia harbor, off Placentia Bay in Newfoundland. Churchill and his aides arrived aboard the battleship *Prince of Wales* while Roosevelt reached the bay on the cruiser *Augusta,* after deceiving the press into believing that he was vacationing on his yacht. Problems of protocol did not complicate the first meeting of the two leaders as the President received the Prime Minister for the first time at a dinner on the American warship.

Military matters were the major subject of the Atlantic Conference, but the attention of the public was to be largely on the Charter. The British brought with them a five-point draft that included some of the ideas of the Four Freedoms speech. The President and Sumner Welles added two additional points, one on the freedom of the seas and the other in support of disarmament and the abandonment of force. In the process of redrafting, the British added a statement dealing with collaboration for improved labor standards, economic growth, and security, which became the fifth point in the final copy.

Two areas of disagreement developed. The Americans wanted the British fourth point to be expanded to include access to markets and raw materials on equal terms and without discrimination. Since this statement could be used as a postwar argument against the British system of imperial preference, Mr. Churchill objected. The term "trade" was subsequently substituted for "markets," and the qualifying phrase "with due regard to their existing obligations" added.

THE ATLANTIC CHARTER

The British Draft

The President of the United States of America and the Prime Minister, Mr. Churchill, representing His Majesty's Government in the United Kingdom, being met together to resolve and concert the means of providing for the safety of their respective countries in face of Nazi and German aggression and of the dangers to all peoples arising therefrom, deem it right to make known certain principles which they both accept for guidance in the framing of their policy and on which they base their hopes for a better future for the world.

FIRST, their countries seek no aggrandizement, territorial or other;

SECOND, they desire to see no territorial changes that do not accord with the freely expressed wishes of the peoples concerned;

THIRD, they respect the right of all peoples to choose the form of government under which they will live; they are only concerned to defend the rights of freedom of speech and of thought without which such choosing must be illusory;

FOURTH, they will strive to bring about a fair and equitable distribution of essential produce not only within their territorial jurisdiction but between the nations of the world.

FIFTH, they seek a peace which will not only cast down forever a Nazi tyranny but by effective international organization will afford to all States and peoples the means of dwelling in security within their own bounds and of traversing the seas and oceans without fear of lawless assault or need of getting burdensome armaments.

The Final Text

Joint declaration of the President of the United States of America and the Prime Minister, Mr. Churchill, representing His Majesty's Government in the United Kingdom, being met together, deem it right to make known certain common principles in the national policies of their respective countries on which they base their hopes for a better future for the world.

FIRST, their countries seek no aggrandizement, territorial or other;

SECOND, they desire to see no territorial changes that do not accord with the freely expressed wishes of the peoples concerned;

THIRD, they respect the right of all peoples to choose the form of government under which they will live; and they wish to see sovereign rights and self-government restored to those who have been forcibly deprived of them;

FOURTH, they will endeavor, with due respect for their existing obligations, to further the enjoyment by all states, great or small, victor or vanquished, of access, on equal terms, to the trade and to the raw materials of the world which are needed for their economic prosperity;

FIFTH, they desire to bring about the fullest collaboration between all nations in the economic field with the object of securing, for all, improved labor standards, economic advancement and social security;

SIXTH, after the final destruction of the Nazi tyranny, they hope to see established a peace which will afford to all nations the means of dwelling in safety within their own boundaries, and which will afford assurance that all the men in all the lands may live out their lives in freedom from fear and want;

SEVENTH, such a peace should enable all men to traverse the high seas and oceans without hindrance;

EIGHTH, they believe that all of the nations of the world, for realistic as well as spiritual reasons, must come to the abandonment of the use of force. Since no future peace can be maintained if land, sea or air armaments continue to be employed by nations which threaten, or may threaten, aggression outside of their frontiers, they believe, pending the establishment of a wider and permanent system of general security, that the disarmament of such nations is essential. They will likewise aid and encourage all other practicable measures which will lighten for peace-loving peoples the crushing burden of armaments.

Secretary of State Hull, with his unwavering faith in the role of free trade as a means to peace, was later to complain that this qualification was a retreat from American principles.

The other area of disagreement was over the words "effective international organization" in the British draft of the fifth point. Roosevelt, skeptical of the worth of any reconstructed League of Nations, was afraid that this point would also stir the opposition of isolationist Americans. He seems to have believed at this time that an Anglo-American police force would be the means of preserving the new *status quo*. Churchill claimed that the British public wanted some assurance of a new world organization. A compromise phrase was consequently included in the final draft, calling for "a wider and permanent system of general security."

Compared to Wilson's Fourteen Points, the Charter lacked specifics. Roosevelt insisted that all matters of detail and treatment of individual nations be deferred until the conclusion of the war. Nor was there anything said about "open diplomacy," that phrase having lost its earlier hopeful connotations.

The impact of two decades of anticolonialism and of growing nationalism was recognized in the inclusion of the phrase "all peoples" in referring to the right of self-determination. But this phrase also had its qualifications. A month after the Atlantic Conference, Prime Minister Churchill told the House of Commons that the choice of the form of government did not apply to peoples who owed allegiance to the British Crown. The drive for independence in India may have been Churchill's chief concern, and he refused the request of the American Ambassador to delete this sentence before delivery.

The term "charter," which the Atlantic document acquired, was a misnomer since there was no grant nor guarantee of rights. As careful readers noted, the authors only expressed their "desire," "wish" and "hope" for the stated objectives. There was a commitment only to the extent that the two leaders were saying that their governments would "seek" and "endeavor" to achieve these ends. Critics on both sides of the Atlantic were also quick to point out the limitations and ambiguities of the statement. The first point accepted past aggrandizement and was only a disclaimer of future gains by nations that already controlled a major share of the earth's resources. The second point on plebiscites, one of Roosevelt's "favorite panaceas," according to Sumner Welles, ignored the demonstrated inadequacy of this device in coping with complex nationality problems. It did not eliminate the grievances of enclaves, and in fractionalizing some political units it created as many difficulties as it tried to remove. To accept the wishes of the peoples concerned also implied that the Greater Germany created by Hitler might be left intact, a prospect that conflicted with the many plans for the weakening of German power.

Point four with its goal of "furthering the enjoyment" on equal terms of access to raw materials required a revolutionized world economy that neither drafter contemplated. Point five and six also called for a more radical attack on sovereignty. Point seven was labeled by British commentators as "an American ritual" since the United States was no longer a weak naval power seeking the rights traditionally associated with "freedom of the seas."

The eighth point, calling for disarmament of potential as well as past aggressors, raised a host of theoretical and practical questions. Who was to identify those who "may threaten"? How were the two allies to disarm other allies? Would the weak be willing to accept disarmament by the strong in the name of general disarmament?

Some dissent was expressed in the United States over the failure of the Charter to include the goal of religious freedom as did the Four Freedoms. Robert Sherwood, on the basis of the Hopkins papers, concluded that this was an "oversight." Roosevelt was sensitive enough to the criticism to act. When the declaration was drafted for all Allies to sign on January 1, 1942, it stated the conviction of the signatories that complete victory made it essential to defend "life, liberty, independence, and religious freedom." The Soviet Ambassador, Maxim Litvinov, preferred the phrase "freedom of conscience," which would cover freedom of nonbelief in nations with a state religion. Roosevelt assured the Ambassador that this freedom was included in "religious freedom," and the American wording was retained.

Criticisms of the Charter continued during the war years, and the President finally replied in a speech made in Ottawa, Canada, in 1943:

> I get everlastingly angry at those who assert vociferously that the Four Freedoms and the Atlantic Charter are nonsense because they are unobtainable. If those people had lived a century and a half ago, they would have sneered and said that the Declaration of Independence was utter piffle. If they had lived nearly a thousand years ago they would have laughed at the ideals of the Magna Carta. And if they had lived several thousand years ago they would have derided Moses when he came from the mountain with the Ten Commandments.

The merits of the Charter hardly ranked with the documents that the President cited effectively in arguing his point. The British government, according to Robert Sherwood, did not regard the statement as "more than a publicity handout." There was no official signed copy; the final text was in the form of mimeographed sheets given to the radio operators for release to the world. The Charter did not acquire any formal character until it was incorporated on January 1, 1942, into what was called "The Declaration of the United Nations." But this did not prevent the Atlantic declaration from becoming a powerful influence on public morale, raising some hopes that a new world based on co-operation would result from the war.

The ideals presented by Churchill and Roosevelt required for their implementation first a victory over an enemy who had at that date over two hundred and fifty experienced and battle-hardened divisions. One of the nations drafting the Charter had already encountered that enemy and had been driven off the Continent. The other had not as yet engaged the enemy and was only slowly mobilizing under the popular assumption that American manpower would not be needed on the continent of Europe. "Give us the weapons and we will finish the job," Churchill had promised Americans.

The only European nation with the manpower to outnumber

the Germans and in direct combat with Hitler's armies on a front of over a thousand miles in length was not a participant in the Atlantic Conference. Sumner Welles reports that there was some discussion of inviting the Soviet Union, but no action was taken.

To the extent that Moscow took recognition of the Churchill-Roosevelt creation, it seemed to view the Charter with suspicion as some form of an Anglo-American scheme for hegemony. When Foreign Minister Anthony Eden conferred with Stalin in December of 1941, Eden refused to discuss details of Eastern European frontiers, saying that Britain was committed to the United States to postpone all such arrangements until the peace conference. In addition, said Eden, the settlements must conform to the ideals of the Atlantic Charter. Stalin said, according to Eden's records, that he was "genuinely surprised."

> I thought that the Atlantic Charter was directed against those people who were trying to establish world dominion. It now looks as if the Charter was directed against the U.S.S.R.

Stalin's interpretation was mistaken. But it was also a great mistake of Roosevelt and Churchill to assume that a victorious Russia could be bound by the 1941 statements of a neutral and a nation that had already suffered a severe defeat at German hands.

4

Roosevelt: The Personal Equation

Franklin Delano Roosevelt has an assured place in history as a great leader of his nation during a period of domestic distress. He was receptive to new ideas, acutely aware of the public temper, and an able handler of men. None of his rivals for the presidency had equal talents. But the talents and techniques that Roosevelt used so effectively on the domestic scene were inadequate for the international problems that he faced. The flexibility and capacity for producing compromises, which were essential in presidential dealings with Congress and conflicting interest groups, had few successes in dealing with the conflicting interests of the Big Three. The imaginativeness with which the New Deal approached the malfunctioning of the economy was lacking in the international sphere or produced ideas so remote from realities as to be irrelevant. The dynamism with which the President collected an array of talent to carry on the battles of 1933 and 1934 was missing from his approach to the diplomatic problems of the war years. The military task alone seemed to exhaust the President and the leadership he assembled.

One of Roosevelt's generally admitted great assets was his personal charm. Aggrieved politicians often left the White House with their problems unresolved, but their loyalty to Roosevelt unshaken. The President was consistently capable of communicating to individuals a strong sense of his good will and his good intentions, enough to divert attention from the failure to achieve whatever the White House mission had been intended to accomplish.

Roosevelt mistakenly assumed that many international problems could also be dissolved by an atmosphere of good fellowship alone. Winston Churchill, another man of charm who loved conversation in a convivial setting, enjoyed his meetings with the President on this level. But the British leader, responsible to a coalition cabinet, had to keep his national objectives more clearly in view. Churchill also knew, as did Foreign Secretary Eden, that some of the issues, which Roosevelt skirted by playing the role of a cordial and entertaining raconteur, still remained when the conversations ended. The Russians, separated from the President and his aides by both language and cultural differences, never responded in any marked degree to this side of the President. Alcohol and extensive toasting was a part of Russian entertainment of diplomats, but it was never used as a substitute for hard bargaining. Roosevelt, on the other hand, was sometimes capable of confusing good fellowship with agreement in principle, thus avoiding the realities of basic differences.

Another characteristic of Roosevelt's was often very effective in domestic matters. Faced with a difficult decision that in any form would be politically costly, the President frequently temporized with the expectation that the situation in time would change in a way that would relieve him of his difficulty. Delay and patience at times were very effective and often the wisest of actions. Not to make some decision in regard to foreign affairs during a war, however, did not always have the same beneficial result. The decision was either left in the hands of the other nation or nations involved, or the sequence of events determined the outcome. Both the British and Russians found this propensity of the White House for delay to be irritating, but also to their own national interests when it permitted them to act on their own. The United States was then faced with a *fait accompli,* difficult, if not impossible, to undo.

Roosevelt's propensity for postponement was accentuated in the latter years of the war as his personal energies flagged and his health declined. Some of his refusals to cope with specific peace problems he was able to justify as avoiding Wilson's plight. In World War II Roosevelt wanted no preliminary "deals" among the Allies to mar the future peace. At a new Versailles the victors could then sit down with a clean slate, with an eye on the principles of the Atlantic Charter, and construct a new world. The American people would have no reason for denouncing their government's tolerance of the evil intrigues of European power politics nor be able to claim that their ideals had been betrayed. At his best, Roosevelt knew that compromises would be necessary, but he had given little thought to the education of the American public to their necessity. And as the gap between the Soviet and American outlook became wider and more obvious in the last year of the war, the President, his physical powers declining rapidly, faced a political task that would have exhausted the intellectual and political energies of the ablest of men.

One other of the President's domestic talents served him ill on the international front. One of his biographers has praised the technique by which he kept the ultimate decision-making power in his own hands. By appointing or assigning several individuals to the same task, by giving his aides ambiguous instructions or uncertain authority, he was able in certain important areas to keep an ambitious man from taking over the responsibilities that belonged to the President. If blunders were made, Roosevelt was still able to avoid direct responsibility while taking credit for successes.

Whatever virtues this technique had in administration, it was a vice in dealing with Great Britain and the Soviet Union. On many important matters, Roosevelt, like some of his predecessors and successors, was determined that the State Department should be in the White House. But he seldom made clear to Secretary Hull the limits of his authority. Hull and his aides frequently discovered that the issue on which they were working was actually being handled by a Presidential agent. The Secretary's role as negotiator was also handicapped by his being an "outsider" in his relations with the White House. At the Moscow Conference in October of 1943, Hull was forced to stall in dealing with Molotov by saying that some matters "required further study" since he was ignorant of the President's views. On other occasions Hull discovered that his ambassadors were dealing directly with the President in communications that did not always reach the Department of State.

Roosevelt's use of Harry Hopkins as his real Secretary of State had its advantages as did Wilson's use of Colonel Edward House. Both men were closely attuned to the President's thinking and had no burden of departmental duties to interfere with their intimate association. But Hopkins' health declined during the war and, on the occasions when he was incapacitated, there was no one who could speak for the President as authoritatively. The resignation of Under Secretary of State Welles in August of 1943 deprived the President of a man whom he trusted and who did have the depth of experience in international affairs that Hopkins lacked.

Without aides who pressed him to undertake this difficult intellectual task, the President never worked seriously and sustainedly on drafting a blueprint for the postwar world that would be acceptable to his two allies and that could also be politically acceptable to the American public. His ideas, to the extent that they have been recorded, were too often nebulous and superficial. During the first year of the coalition, at least, he did not see the complications of the Big Three differences. "Winston and I will write the Peace Treaty," he told his Secretary of the Treasury in 1942. Knowing something of British economic weakness and increasing dependence on Lend-Lease aid, he probably assumed that Britain would be the junior partner in the peacemaking task. The Soviet Union, presumably, if it survived the war, would be too involved in national reconstruction to play a major role in creating a new world.

These were the loose and shaky premises on which the White

House based whatever consideration was given to peace-planning in 1942, and in 1943 prior to the first Big Three encounter. The military operation of the war and the associated domestic problems left little time and energy for thinking about the postwar arrangements. During the first two years of American participation in the war, Churchill crossed the Atlantic four times to confer with Roosevelt while the latter crossed the Atlantic once to North Africa for the Casablanca Conference of January 1943. The two men also corresponded frequently and lengthily. But the task of defeating the Axis powers and the complications of their frequently tense relations with the Soviet Union had the highest priorities. Their talk of the future international order was in vague terms and often incidental.

The Soviet Union took the first initiative in trying to negotiate specific wartime settlements and at a time when victory still seemed a very remote possibility. Stalin in early November of 1941 turned from the immediate military tasks to raise with Churchill the question of the postwar organization of the peace. Unless there was some understanding on this point as well as on their military co-operation, Stalin said that there could be no mutual trust. At that date Kiev had fallen to the Germans, Moscow and Leningrad were threatened, and the prospects for defeating the Germans were slim. To want to discuss the future peace at that point took considerable optimism.

In part the Soviet initiative may have come out of Stalin's strong distrust for British motives, a distrust which at least equaled that of Churchill when he considered his Communist eastern partner. Both Marxist dogma and Hitler's tactics encouraged the Soviet leader to expect a change of face in London when the German crusade against the Bolshevik menace to Europe was certain of success. The Munich settlement's open disregard for Soviet interests was not to be quickly forgotten. Ambassador Maisky in London could also have exaggerated the strength of anti-Communist sentiment among the British ruling classes. The Kremlin had been surprised by British determination to continue the war against Germany, once Hitler turned to the east, and the fear of an Anglo-

German front against Russia was never completely dispelled until the war was over.

Before making his appeal to Churchill, Stalin spoke about the problems of the peace with Lord Beaverbrook and Averell Harriman when the two envoys visited the Kremlin in late September of 1941. He then proposed that the Anglo-Russian wartime alliance, signed on July 12, 1941, be extended to a postwar alliance as well. Stalin was also concerned about the assessment of war damages on the Germans. Lord Beaverbrook was not authorized to discuss peace terms and only reminded the Russian leader of the Atlantic Charter's eight principles. Stalin's reply was, "What about getting the Germans to pay for the damage?" an issue untouched by the Anglo-American proclamation.

On his way back to the United States, Harriman warned Foreign Minister Eden that Stalin would be offended if he had no response to his overture for a postwar alliance. Britain was not ready for such a step, nor ready to promise an invasion that would divert German strength from the hard-pressed Russian Front. The result was a blunt message from Stalin, on November 8, 1941, complaining that the British had failed to declare war on Germany's allies, Finland, Hungary, and Rumania. Stalin said that this was "intolerable" and that the arms shipments coming from Britain were arriving in a state of disrepair. Again Stalin pointed to the necessity of agreement on the peace if there was to be mutual trust.

Churchill's reaction was one of anger, and he refused to reply. After two weeks of silence Stalin sent a note to soften his previous statement. This brought an assurance to Stalin from London that Communism was "not an obstacle to our making a good plan for our mutual safety and rightful interests." Eden was subsequently sent to Moscow in December to take up the issues that Stalin raised.

When the British Foreign Secretary reached Moscow on December 16, the attack on Pearl Harbor, followed by Germany's declaration of war, had made the United States a legal belligerent in Europe and Asia. The Russians now feared that American resources, beginning to flow to their aid through the Lend-Lease program, would be diverted to the Pacific campaigns of the United States. There was also fear that the Anglo-American partnership, now consummated, would as a matter of tactics delay peace discussions until they had achieved a strong military position in Europe. Eden was faced with two Russian draft treaties, one for a military alliance, the second to provide for co-operation in dealing with postwar questions. To the second treaty was attached a secret protocol to settle the future frontiers of Eastern Europe.

For the Russians, the forfeiture to the Poles after World War I of Russian-speaking portions of White Russia and the Ukraine was a great loss. The recovery of these areas was not only a matter of national pride, but also considered important for security. Stalin proposed to Eden that the future boundary with Poland should follow basically that proposed by the British in 1919, the so-called Curzon line. Poland was to be compensated for this loss by expansion westward at the expense of Germany. Stalin also claimed for the Soviet Union the retention of the territory of the three Baltic states created in 1919, Latvia, Lithuania, and Estonia, which the Soviet Union had absorbed in 1940, as well as Bessarabia, which had been taken from Rumania. In regard to Finland, Stalin proposed retaining the boundary established by the Russo-Finnish peace terms of 1940 along with the right to establish bases on Finland's Baltic coast. For the rest of Eastern Europe, the Russians were willing to see a return to the 1938 frontiers with Czechoslovakia and Austria restored as independent states.

Stalin also urged that agreements be reached on the imposition of reparations on Germany and that some scheme of partition be developed that would prevent the Germans from posing any future military threat. Peace and order would be kept in Europe by a council of the victorious powers with a military force at its disposal. Some European states might be permitted to federate in their own interest.

Eden was only able to respond to Stalin's specific proposals with a plea for delay even though he was in agreement with some of the measures. Before leaving for Moscow the British Foreign

Secretary had received a strong warning from Cordell Hull against making any specific agreements with the Russians on the future of Europe. Churchill, when he had received word of the Russian terms while en route to the United States, had reinforced the Hull warning and rejected Stalin's boundary proposals as violations of the principles of the Atlantic Charter. When Eden raised the question of the Charter with Stalin, the Russian leader would have none of it: "A declaration I regard as algebra, but an agreement as practical arithmetic. I do not wish to decry algebra, but I prefer practical arithmetic."

Stalin thought in terms of traditional spheres of influence in his proposals for Eastern Europe, and he was ready to grant Britain a similar measure of freedom to take what steps she considered necessary to achieve security in Western Europe. He was not opposed, he said, to British bases in Norway and Sweden. If France did not enter the peace as a major power, he thought Britain should have bases on the French coast as well as in Belgium and the Netherlands. Furthermore, he wanted the agreements now. He remembered what he considered the shabby treatment Russia had received from the western powers in the intra-war period and, as he told Premier Sikorski of the Polish Government in Exile a few days before Eden arrived, he could not be sure that when the war ended Russia would not again be treated as a "poor relation." A compromise was even offered that avoided specific mention of boundaries but bound Britain and Russia to work for European reconstruction after the war "with full regard to the interests of the U.S.S.R. in the restitution of its frontiers violated by the Hitlerite aggression." Since this in effect meant the 1941 boundaries, Eden refused to accept an indirect commitment that might arouse American opposition. Stalin insisted that the boundary questions would have to be settled in the immediate future. As Eden left Moscow, he wired Churchill that "we must expect continued badgering on this issue."

While Eden was in Moscow an eager Churchill was on his way to Washington, carrying drafts of papers to convert Americans to his visions of the "Grand Strategy" by which the war would be henceforth fought. He felt that he could now talk bluntly to the full partners in the war. He had conferred with the Chiefs of Staff before leaving London and when they urged some caution, he said, with a wicked leer, as General Brooke remembered it, "Oh! That is the way we talked to her while we were wooing her; now that she is in the harem, we talk to her quite differently." Most of Churchill's thoughts were directed towards military matters including the creation of an Anglo-American military committee henceforth known as the Combined Chiefs of Staff to co-ordinate strategy. No consideration seems to have been given to an effort to get the Russians to participate in this body. As the Prime Minister stated in one of his drafts, he favored continuing aid to the U.S.S.R.: "In this way alone shall we hold our influence over Stalin and be able to weave the mighty Russian effort into the general texture of the war." It was an optimistic assumption to make in view of Eden's Moscow conversations.

The major American diplomatic contribution to this Roosevelt-Churchill conference, code-named ARCADIA, was a declaration to be signed by all allied powers, whom Roosevelt suggested should be known as the United Nations. The signatories were to subscribe to "a common program of purposes and principles" embodied in the Atlantic Charter. To avoid involvement with the Senate, Roosevelt wanted this clearly not to be a treaty that required ratification, and at first he objected to the inclusion of a pledge not to conclude a separate peace. The State Department's legal advice was that this did not make the declaration into a treaty.

The inclusion of the goal of religious freedom had been preceded by Harriman's efforts in Moscow to persuade Stalin to reduce restrictions on religious freedom, with American public opinion in mind. Stalin finally gave some assurance of liberalization, but Foreign Minister Molotov was concerned about the way in which this point was being added to meet domestic political needs. In conversation with Harriman, Molotov suggested that Roosevelt was not as religious a man as he claimed to be. The President learned of this and later amused Churchill by reporting a long talk he'd had with Ambassador Litvinov about his soul and the dangers of hell-fire. Churchill replied in the same vein by offering Roosevelt the position of Archbishop of Canterbury if he lost the next election.

This banter between the two leaders did not avoid a clash of interests when the issue of India was raised. The Americans proposed including that country as a signatory among the United Nations. The British rejected any Indian claims to sovereignty and held that the signature of the British sovereign included India. The anticolonial feelings of the United States on the Indian question were strong, and Churchill finally conceded on this point. Another British concession accepted the refusal of the United States to invite the Free French movement led by General Charles de Gaulle to sign along with other governments in exile. The United States still recognized the Vichy regime in France, and de Gaulle offended Secretary Hull by seizing control of two French islands off the coast of Newfoundland in the name of the Free French. The American position kept France off the United Nations Declaration until December of 1944, when Paris was once more in French hands with de Gaulle in power.

The classic problems of protocol were raised when it came to signing the United Nations Declaration. Roosevelt decided that Britain, China, Russia, and the United States would become the primary signatories. Britain waived alphabetical precedence, and the United States signed first, followed by Britain, the Soviet Union, and China. The remaining signatories were called to the State Department a day later, on January 2, 1942, to sign in alphabetical order. Eight of the signatories represented governments in exile, claiming to speak for states under German occupation. Some embarrassment developed when representatives of the three Baltic nations absorbed by the Soviet Union offered to adhere and other "free groups" claiming to represent Germany, Rumania, and Korea attempted to secure a form of recognition by an act of adherence. The Russians were suspicious of this move, and with the support of Churchill the fringe groups were excluded.

THE UNITED NATIONS DECLARATION

The Governments signatory hereto,

Having subscribed to a common program of purposes and principles embodied in the Joint Declaration of the President of the United States of America and the Prime Minister of the United Kingdom of Great Britain and Northern Ireland dated August 14, 1941, known as the Atlantic Charter,

Being convinced that complete victory over their enemies is essential to defend life, liberty, independence and religious freedom, and to preserve human rights and justice in their own lands as well as in other lands, and that they are now engaged in a common struggle against savage and brutal forces seeking to subjugate the world, Declare:

(1) Each Government pledges itself to employ its full resources, military or economic, against those members of the Tripartite Pact and its adherents with which such government is at war.

(2) Each Government pledges itself to cooperate with the Governments signatory hereto and not to make a separate armistice or peace with the enemies.

The foregoing declaration may be adhered to by other nations which are, or which may be, rendering material assistance and contributions in the struggle for victory over Hitlerism.

Washington, January 1, 1942.

Basically the United Nations Declaration was, as Secretary Hull states in his memoirs, an effort "to try to bind all the nations" to the Atlantic Charter and to commit them "in advance to certain principles" while leaving specific details to consideration at the end of the war. Churchill was strongly urged while in Washington to resist completely Russian efforts to reach agreements on Eastern Europe. But when the Prime Minister returned to London he was again faced with the Russian proposals. The military situation was also shifting. The Russians were, surprisingly, surviving through the first winter of the war while the loss of Singapore in February of 1942 was for Britain "the greatest disaster in our history" as Churchill saw it at the time. The Russian resistance to the expected German spring offensive became increasingly important as the setbacks faced in Asia put additional limits on the aid that Britain and the United States could extend to their ally.

Foreign Secretary Eden reviewed Britain's dilemma for the Cabinet late in January of 1942. He pointed out that if Germany were eventually defeated and France remained a weak power, there would be no counterweight to Russia in Europe. Soviet influence could be expected to spread across the Continent and Communist governments to come into being in the majority of states. It seemed self-evident then that Russia would not be willing to accept in victory frontiers that were short of those held at the time of the German attack. While admitting that Soviet policies were basically amoral, Eden said that the American policy was exaggeratedly moral, at least where non-American interests were concerned. It was unrealistic and not to British interests to create problems in relations with the Soviet Union by opposing what the Russians would do regardless of protests. Eden did not want his country to have to choose between the United States and the Soviet Union; Washington would have to be the first choice, but that difficulty could be avoided by a sensible compromise.

The Foreign Secretary outlined two sets of concessions, either of which he hoped would satisfy the Russians and yet not incur an American veto. The first was to pledge British support at a future peace conference for Soviet claims to military bases on the soil of neighboring nations in the Black Sea and Baltic Sea area. The Americans, Eden wrote, had used military bases on foreign soil for their own security and might understand the Soviet use of the same devices. If the Russians accepted this approach, they were also to be given to understand that it did not preclude their claims to absorb the Baltic countries as well as Bessarabia, the annexed section of Rumania, and the Finnish cession of 1940.

If the first proposal was too strong for the Americans, Eden suggested a British pledge of support for future Soviet control of the foreign policy and defense of the Baltic states, a method of achieving security without complete absorption. Washington was fully informed of these proposals, as they had been of all the conversations with the Russians, and by the end of March the British Cabinet decided to go ahead with the Russian negotiations.

Secretary Hull was a major center of resistance to approving any British arrangements with the Russians on Eastern Europe. He reviewed the American position for the President in a long memorandum on February 4, 1942. Any arrangements before the peace conference, Hull claimed, would weaken the alliance against Hitler and introduce mutual suspicions among the member states while only temporarily improving relations with the Soviet Union. A compromise on principles, Hull believed, would only lead to further and more far-reaching Russian demands and have an unfortunate effect on the small countries and on all those opposed to "the spread of Bolshevism." Hull apparently had in mind the governments in exile from Eastern Europe whose representatives were steady pleaders for their case and who often expressed as much fear of Russia as of the Germany which had occupied their countries.

Under Secretary of State Welles supported Hull's position for the most part. Like Hull, Welles had something of a Wilsonian vision of a new Europe, free from what Welles called "the shoddy, inherently vicious kind of patch-work world order" that had been constructed between 1919 and 1939. When the British Ambassador, Lord Halifax, spoke of the need of the Soviet Union to constitute an element in the balance of power against any future rise of Germany, Welles saw this as evidence of the continuance of "the worst phase of the spirit of Munich." To prevent the rise of a dangerous new Germany, Welles proposed a return to the weak federation of German states created in 1815, with Prussia removed from its once dominant role.

Ambassador Halifax tried to counter the State Department by warning that a rejection of the Russian boundary proposals might end any hope for fruitful co-operation. The Russians, he said, could easily have asked for more in the traditional areas of their national interest: control of the Dardanelles, spheres of influence in the Balkans, access to the Persian Gulf, and even access to the Atlantic through Norway. This type of argument left the State

Department cold. Denunciations of British policy became strong. Assistant Secretary of State Adolf Berle saw London's plans as "a Baltic Munich" while Welles damned them as "indefensible from every moral standpoint, but likewise extraordinarily stupid." Roosevelt, on the other hand, told Halifax that he could see no reason for worry about the Baltic states; if the Russians were strong enough militarily to reoccupy them, neither the United States nor Britain could or would turn them out. But the President was unwilling to have that realistic prospect recorded on paper. This was Roosevelt's way of playing safe with American public opinion and preserving the illusion that the future peace would be purely Wilsonian, free from concessions to national interests. Eden thought that this was the worst possible solution, neither strengthening relations with Russia nor blocking the extension of Soviet power.

Roosevelt's position, in historical perspective so short-sighted, was fortified by the President's confidence in his ability to win Stalin over to the American point of view. Churchill, who in January of 1942 felt that acceptance of Russian expansion in Eastern Europe would "dishonour our cause," by March felt that the importance of good relations with the Kremlin was an overriding consideration. The Atlantic Charter, he cabled the President, should not be construed so as to deny the Russians the frontiers they held when Germany attacked. And on March 9 he informed Stalin that he was urging Roosevelt to approve the signing of a treaty on Russia's future frontiers. The President's response was a sharp cable in which he said that he was going to be "brutally frank."

> I think I can personally handle Stalin better than either your Foreign Office or my State Department. Stalin hates the guts of all your top people. He thinks he likes me better and I hope he will continue to do so.

Churchill in his memoirs makes no comment on what must surely have been seen as an act of great arrogance on the part of Roosevelt. Halifax continued to appeal for American acceptance of the Russian treaty until Sumner Welles told him on April 1 that Roosevelt could see no useful purpose in further discussion.

The President then made his own approach to Stalin in an effort to divert the boundary settlement. On April 12 the Soviet Premier received an invitation to spend a few days with the President during the coming summer "near our common border off Alaska." In the meantime the President said he had "a very important military proposal," using American forces to relieve the Russian Front, and asked that Molotov and a Russian general be sent to Washington to discuss it. The President believed, as Hopkins said, that this "should take the heat off Russia's diplomatic demands upon England."

In the meantime the British Foreign Office continued to seek modifications in the proposed agreements to make the final treaty more acceptable to Washington. The Russians were again asked to exclude completely the Polish boundary question and to promise that peoples in the Baltic states would be free to move out from Russian rule. This continued attempt to water down the text created the same irritations in Moscow that Washington was expressing for the opposite reasons. Molotov's visit was consequently delayed, and he did not arrive in London until May 20, with his appointment in Washington to follow.

After almost a week of conferring, a Russo-British treaty was signed on May 26, 1942. It said nothing at all about the disputed boundary questions and instead bound the two governments to a twenty-year alliance by which both nations were "to work together in close and friendly collaboration after the establishment of peace." This represented a major reversal of the Russian position. Welles told Ambassador Halifax that he thought the change in text was "a miracle."

Why did the Russians make such a drastic diplomatic retreat from a goal that they set shortly after the German attack opened the question of future borders? Eden found the Russian motives "obscure" but saw the overriding purpose of the Soviet Union as the opening of a Second Front in Europe as soon as possible. Going to Washington to discuss Roosevelt's "very important military proposal," with an inoffensive treaty with Britain, would surely facilitate American action. Molotov had said on his arrival in London that the Second Front was more important than the proposed treaty and that the latter might better be postponed if Britain could not accept the minimal Soviet conditions. There may have been hints by Roosevelt in his conversations with Ambassador Litvinov that a treaty absorbing the Baltic countries and part of Poland would so outrage American opinion as to make difficult a cross-Channel invasion to relieve the Russian Front.

The Soviet Foreign Minister arrived secretly in Washington on May 29 and began his conversations directly with the President. Molotov was told to inform Stalin that the Americans "expect the formation of a second front this year." The American communiqué, released when Molotov had returned home, stated that "full understanding was reached with regard to the urgent tasks of creating a second front in Europe in 1942." General George Marshall, who had taken part in some of the conversation, felt that the wording was too strong and that the date 1942 should be omitted in view of great problems still to be solved in mounting so early an offensive. But Roosevelt was unwilling to permit military realities to interfere with his political objectives and overruled his Chief of Staff.

The President also talked with Molotov at length about the nature of the postwar international organization, leaving the first extensive record of his views as noted by Harry Hopkins and the American translator Professor Samuel Cross of Harvard. In contrast to the Wilsonian position that he held against wartime territorial settlements, Roosevelt broke quite completely with the idea of the League of Nations. The Europe based on the ideals of the Atlantic Charter was to be run on the more conservative classic concepts of Vienna of 1815. The Quadruple Alliance, created then to maintain the peace against a revival of an aggressive France, was revived in Roosevelt's idea of a four-power alliance, not only to police Europe, but the world. The new alliance was not only to make the rules but enforce them. It would go much further than the Quadruple Alliance was prepared to in violating the sovereignty of the other nations. The four policemen—the United States, Britain, Russia, and China—were to disarm the rest of the world and keep other states in this condition by means of inspection. The policemen were also to be prepared to blockade and bomb nations that menaced the peace.

The Russian Foreign Minister seems to have been somewhat taken back by Roosevelt's sweeping generalizations on how the new world would be run. He asked the President if these views represented his "final and considered judgment," to which Roosevelt replied affirmatively. When questioned about details, however, the President was willing to make some modifications in what he called "a brand new approach to world peace." Molotov asked about keeping France disarmed; Roosevelt said this should be that nation's initial condition, but at a later date France might become one of the policemen. The great danger, Roosevelt said, would be in having too many policemen. Molotov expressed some concern about the status of lesser powers like Poland and Turkey, whose prestige would suffer greatly if excluded from the Big Four. Roosevelt felt that they could be "nominally" partners in the police work and that other friendly nations might receive the same status. He was unwilling to visualize, however, another League of Nations with a hundred members. This was quite in contrast to the United Nations Declaration of the previous January, which promised equality to all nations. Molotov could not have been other than confused by this President who had just taken such a strong position as the defender of the small nations of Eastern Europe and then talked of subordinating them completely to Big Four control. One qualification was made in respect to the policemen: China would acquire membership only if a strong central government was created.

The Big Four would end imperialism by taking away many islands and colonial possessions from "weak nations" and having them governed by some form of international trusteeship. The President wanted an arrangement that avoided the limitations of the League mandate system, which gave the mandatory nation virtual sovereignty, "the most elaborate fig leaf ever devised for imperialism," in the words of A. J. P. Taylor, the British historian. Specifically the President mentioned the Japanese-mandated islands of the Pacific—the Marshalls, Marianas, and Carolines—French Indo-China, the Malay States, the Dutch East Indies and Siam. Since Siam had a good claim to being sovereign for some centuries and since the Malay States were the colonial possessions of one of the policemen, Great Britain, some obvious complications would beset the President's scheme. The peace as a whole, Roosevelt said, would likely be a dictated one, but so administered as to be acceptable to the people of the aggressor nations.

Molotov immediately reported Roosevelt's views to Moscow and told the President before he left Washington that Stalin was fully in accord with him. The Russians, sorely pressed by the renewed German offensive and "a bit down in the mouth," as Roosevelt told Churchill, saw the promise of a second front as being of far more immediate importance. Molotov visited London again on his return trip, bringing what Eden called "an explosive message" in the form of the promised invasion of Europe in 1942. Unconsulted by Roosevelt, the British felt that he had gone too far in raising Russian hopes for an action that they did not believe possible. All the difficulties of an invasion in 1942 were explained to Molotov along with an *aide-mémoire* that Churchill felt absolved the Allies from any firm commitment.

A desperate Russia preferred to take Roosevelt's promise at its face value and disregard the British qualifications. The British Ambassador wrote from Moscow that Molotov had returned "a new man" and that the Russian government had become far more co-operative as a result of his mission. The American Ambassador Admiral Standley also reported a new enthusiasm as the prospect of relief from the full weight of the German offensive forces seemed imminent. But, warned Standley, "if such a second front does not materialize quickly and on a large scale, these people will be so deluded in their belief in our sincerity of purpose and will for concerted action that inestimable harm will be done to the cause of the United Nations." Molotov made the same point to the British and American ambassadors in talking of what he called the

"Anglo-Saxon promises," which could bring cruel disillusionment if unredeemed.

When Churchill went to Moscow in August of 1942 to announce that there would be no landing in Europe until 1943, Stalin and his aides were bitter over that they considered betrayal and the withdrawal of a *quid pro quo.* Thoughts of capitalist intrigue, of Munich, and of all the other sources of Russian Communist distrust of the Western powers were easily revived. The value of Roosevelt's tactic, as it seems to have been—to stall the discussion of boundary questions with the Soviet Union by promising a major military action that the United States and Britain were unprepared to undertake, even in 1943 as it turned out—must be seriously questioned. Domestic considerations may have been the major reason for Roosevelt's action, a determination that the cry of betrayal and "secret treaties" could never again be raised against a Democratic administration as they had been against Woodrow Wilson. If this was the President's rationale for overriding the cautions of his military advisers, he was only postponing the day when Americans would see the European struggle in a more realistic light and realize that national interests still dominated European national policies as they did American.

5

The Military Perimeters of the Peace

The map of Europe and of Asia in 1945 was not drawn by the peace planners alone; it was also the product of the military history of the previous five years. The location of the world's military forces at the moment when the last shots were fired in some areas overruled the aspirations and intentions of the political leaders. In some instances military achievements defined the perimeters within which the peacemakers had to work. And war policies worked in opposition to many peace policies.

For Great Britain the peace goals far exceeded the nation's military capacities. The experience of World War I set narrow limits on the will to sacrifice in any task other than driving an invader back into the sea. Approximately a million men died under the British flag before the war ended in 1918, almost ten percent of the male population of military age. The truth of one of Wilfred Owen's last poems was clear to the survivors:

> This is the thing they know and never speak,
> That England one by one had fled to France.
> Not many elsewhere now, save under France.

No British government was prepared to exhaust the nation and destroy the leaders of a new generation of youth in another world conflict.

French leaders had similar misgivings about risking another decimation of their population. France had lost over 1.3 million, approximately eighteen percent of the military age males, between 1914 and 1918. This was a physical and intellectual loss too great to repeat.

Britain and France as a consequence of their earlier experience approached World War II with a defensive outlook that determined their military strategy. Before 1940 no serious consideration was given in London to the mobilization of enough manpower and resources to conduct a major land war in Europe against Germany. British military and political opinion was generally in accord that such an attempt would be folly. No preparations were made for the dispatch of any expeditionary force to France until a few months before the outbreak of war in 1939. Only in February of that year did the British Cabinet decide that a part of the Regular Army should be equipped to fight on the Continent. The basic national strategy was to defend the home islands and the Empire.

French military strategy was tied to the Maginot line. It was expected to present an impassable barrier to any German attack, a vast fort from which the French Army could fight in security. Never again would the poilu die by the thousands as great waves of men tried to cross "no man's land" and drive out the Boche invader. The most dangerous effect of the great French fortification was a psychological one, as described by British General Alan Brooke, who visited it in the spring of 1940. He felt that "a sense of false security is engendered, a feeling of sitting behind an impregnable iron fence, and should the fence perchance be broken, the French fighting spirit might well be brought crumbling with it." But even Winston Churchill wrote before 1940 of the Maginot line as "a wise and prudent measure."

Out of these defensive postures a victory was eventually expected. British strategic thought saw Germany crumbling under a war of attrition in which the British Navy with its dominance of the seas eventually strangled the Nazi economy. It was hoped that civil disorders would follow, breaking the morale of the German

Army, and eliminating the need for protracted ground conflict. This sort of optimism supported the inclination to disturb the peacetime way of life as little as possible. At the end of six months of war, Britain had still called to arms only one out of every forty-eight military-age males compared to one out of eight then in uniform in France.

Paradoxically, a certain pessimism also contributed to the initial failure to launch a major mobilization. In the Spanish Civil War (1936–39), German bombers demonstrated how devastating small-scale operations could be. Many expected World War II to begin with an Armageddon in which swarms of bombers destroyed major population centers. The British Air Staff estimated in May of 1939 that the German *Luftwaffe* could maintain an attack on London of a thousand bombers daily for two weeks. Since both British and French air forces lagged far behind the German, reprisals offered little hope of compensation. The two Allies consequently engaged their energies in building ground defenses while encouraging restraints on air action. The British and French staffs agreed in March of 1939 not to initiate air attacks "against any but purely 'military' objectives in the narrowest sense of the word." When the expected German air attacks on London and Paris did not come in the fall of 1939, Allied bombers were confined to dropping propaganda leaflets over Germany and to some minor attacks on German naval establishments. Although the *Luftwaffe* was used against Warsaw effectively, it was only after the German raid on Rotterdam, May 14, 1940, killing nearly a thousand civilians, that British bombers began striking at a wide range of targets in Germany.

The fall of France and the British flight at Dunkerque was a blow to the illusions of optimism. "The blunt fact is that Britain cannot now reconquer the Continent and we are not going to do so," Assistant Secretary of State Adolf Berle told Cordell Hull in July of 1940. British leaders had difficulty in not agreeing with Berle's first point. The possibility of victory without defeating the German Army looked remote. But Britain would have to build an invasion force from its population of approximately 47 million to fight a Germany of 80 million, further strengthened by the forced labor of the occupied countries. Only two nations had population and industrial resources great enough to build the armed superiority necessary to overwhelm Hitler's might. One was the Soviet Union with its 1939 population of approximately 170 million, and the other was the United States with some 132 million. If either could be drawn into the conflict and add their divisions to the British armies, the destruction of the Reich's ground forces was possible.

The importance of military victory loomed so great that London could do little to question the price that an alliance with either of these powers would demand. The most clear-sighted proponent of the von Clausewitz viewpoint would have had difficulty arguing that political considerations should take precedence over the military in a nation that feared an invasion by the greatest European army assembled since Napoleonic times. But it was necessary to recognize, nevertheless, that military exigencies would mean that some political goals were no longer obtainable, that the choice of means available was limited, and that these means would influence the ends sought.

An alliance with the United States was Britain's greatest hope and one that would require the least in the way of compromises of national interests. The Churchill Cabinet felt a certain kinship with the Roosevelt administration and, as the Atlantic Charter demonstrated, agreement could be reached on broad principles. But there were also clashing interests. The traditional hostility of the United States toward the British Empire remained strong and was a factor no American administration could ignore. Roosevelt himself was unsympathetic to Churchill's goal of preserving the imperial political relationship on its prewar basis. Cordell Hull was determined to attack the empire's economic ties in the form of imperial preference. And most informed Americans had great sympathies with the aspirations of Mohandas Gandhi and other Indian nationalists for independence. Yet, as Churchill frequently affirmed, His Majesty's Government believed that the preservation of the British Empire was an essential aspect of national survival and a major goal of the war effort.

An Anglo-Russian alliance clearly offered even greater difficulties for Britain. Against two powerful enemies, Napoleonic France and Imperial Germany, Britain and Russia had fought together as valuable allies. But in the century between these two wars their interests had clashed repeatedly and even produced one conflict, the Crimean War, out of which Britain and France gained for a time a demilitarization of the Black Sea. The Russian threat to the British "lifeline" to India and to India itself, while composed largely of myths and misunderstandings, was deeply ingrained in British strategic thought. On the other hand, against a Prussian or German enemy, Russia was the only major country in a geographic position to open a vast second front.

Prime Minister Churchill, despite his long personal hostility to Russian Communism, believed that his predecessor, Chamberlain, had been mistaken in his coolness in dealing with Moscow. In the debate that followed the British unilateral action in giving a guarantee to Poland in April of 1939, Churchill had noted that he was unwilling to ask favors of Moscow, but:

> I beg His Majesty's Government to get some of these brutal truths into their heads. Without an effective eastern front there can be no satisfactory defence of our interests in the west, and without Russia there can be no effective eastern front.

Whether these truths were brutal or not, the Chamberlain government failed to offer an Anglo-Russian alliance on terms that might have prevented the Nazi-Soviet pact.

When Churchill came to power, the need for an eastern front was even more pressing, and he made some efforts to draw Moscow away from its uneasy relationship with Berlin. Stalin made no favorable response. As a beleaguered island with its forces driven from the Continent, Britain, in the eyes of the Soviet leader, had little to offer to Russian security compared to the Berlin pact, which at least postponed the showdown. When the war came

Stalin knew that it would take the full strength of Russian manpower and that the contribution of Britain would be a minor one.

When Hitler launched his attack eastward in the summer of 1941, London welcomed Russian involvement. British military experts, like the American, doubted that the Red Army would long continue to fight. Communist-led fighting forces were thought to be inherently weak, a conviction reinforced by Russian difficulties in crushing their small Finnish opponent. But Churchill welcomed Russia as an ally who would, as he wrote, "spare a lot of English blood." He told his secretary, "If Hitler invaded Hell I would make at least a favorable reference to the Devil in the House of Commons." On that practical basis, Britain joined Communist Russia in an alliance against Nazism, an ideology that Churchill found "indistinguishable from the worst features of Communism."

London continued to woo its other potential ally. An Anglo-French military staff in April of 1939 recommended that in the event of war, efforts be made to secure "the active assistance of the United States or at least benevolent neutrality." During the period of the "Phony War," the neutrality soon became benevolent as Roosevelt secured a change in the Neutrality Law that made possible the continued purchase of arms from the United States on a "cash and carry" basis.

When Churchill took office in May of 1940 he devoted some of his boundless energies to trying to draw the United States into full participation in the European War. While Roosevelt shared the Prime Minister's conviction that Nazi Germany must be destroyed in the interests of the security of the United States as well as Britain, he was unwilling to face the implications of that conviction. He was also inhibited by the strong antiwar and isolationist sentiment of the American public. Although the majority of Americans were sympathetic with Britain, only a small minority were prepared to pay the human and economic price that a new expeditionary force would require.

A tug of war took place between London and Washington

between May of 1940 and December of 1941 with Churchill, by a variety of appeals, trying to secure either an American declaration of war or a series of steps clearly leading to war. As France collapsed, London claimed that only immediate American action could save Britain's ally. After the French armistice, Churchill warned of the dangers of the loss of the British fleet if the United States did not begin trans-Atlantic military operations. But Roosevelt in the summer and fall of 1940 was fighting for an unprecedented third term against critics who charged him with covertly leading the nation to war. Both presidential candidates assured the voters that no American boys would be sent to fight on European soil. It was a bold enough step for the President to transfer fifty World War I destroyers to Britain in August of 1940 in exchange for ninety-nine-year leases to bases on British territory in the Western Hemisphere. Churchill wrote that this "decidedly unneutral action" justified a German declaration of war on the United States, but Hitler was unwilling at this time to extend his operations.

In December of 1940 Churchill made a lengthy appeal for financial aid since British reserves were being exhausted by large purchases of American arms and supplies. By this date a substantial share of the economic recovery of the United States and decline in unemployment was directly related to British orders. Domestic as well as foreign policy considerations combined to urge that this trade relationship be maintained. Roosevelt's response was the Lend-Lease Bill, introduced in Congress in January of 1941 and passed in March. Authorization was provided by which Britain, the Soviet Union, China, France, and smaller nations were eventually to draw on the United States for approximately $50 billion to secure arms, munitions, food, and other matériel.

As the United States came closer to entry into the war in 1941, the pace of mobilization remained an almost leisurely one. The White House, like the British government in 1939, delayed facing up to the needs of another American expeditionary force. Churchill was in part responsible for preserving American complacency. In a broadcast made in February of 1941 the Prime

Minister spoke to reassure the American Congress, which was then debating the implications of the Lend-Lease Bill. He said that the conflict was "not a war of vast armies."

> We do not need the gallant armies which are forming throughout the American Union. We do not need them this year, nor the next year, nor any year that I can foresee.

The final famous line was "Give us the tools and we will finish the job," a statement that he later admitted in his memoirs could only be "an interim pronouncement." The Prime Minister felt that he had at this time to quiet American fears by implying that the war was going to be won without blood, sweat, and tears on the part of the people of the United States. At the Atlantic Conference in August of 1941, Churchill still talked about victory without involving large armies. When the peoples of Europe were ready to throw off their Nazi rulers, a few armored divisions would be landed with the most modern equipment to speed the transition. Even armies of occupation would be unnecessary, Churchill told Roosevelt, since liberated areas could be quickly turned over to indigenous anti-Nazi forces.

Although as late as September of 1941 Roosevelt appeared to accept the optimistic view of Churchill, his military advisers knew better. American military planners saw little reason for believing that Germany would be defeated without the creation of a large invasion force. Assuming the defeat of the Soviet Union, as was common until late in 1941—the scale of the American task was recognized as gigantic. The earliest date at which it was estimated that an invasion could take place was the summer of 1943. By that date the German forces were expected to mount up to 400 divisions. According to classic doctrine, invading forces needed a two-to-one superiority for success. If Britain could squeeze 100 divisions from its manpower pool, this would still require 700 divisions from the United States and a total mobilization of 22 million men.

When the effect of withdrawing 22 million men from the

American economy was examined, it was obvious that it would require many sacrifices that too many would be unwilling to make. Only if the nation faced a direct military threat to its own shores could the public be expected to accept such a drastic dislocation of the normal patterns and standards of living. Consequently the estimates of the military planners had to be revised in terms of what was politically possible. Mobilization goals were cut 10 million, to aim at approximately 9 percent of the 1940 United States population, or 12 million. The Army was allocated 8.5 million and the remainder of the manpower assigned to the Navy and the air arms of both services. To make an invasion successful with little more than half the estimated manpower, the military planners turned their attention to higher degrees of mechanization and to the technical improvement of weaponry as compensatory factors.

Before the Pearl Harbor attack, little progress was made on the lowered manpower goal. A one-year Selective Service Act, passed in September of 1940, provided for the training of 1.2 million inductees and 800 thousand reserves. In August of 1941 the conscription system was extended for eighteen months, but the legislation passed the House of Representatives with only a one-vote majority, an indication of the strength of public pressures against a large-scale mobilization. When the Japanese struck at Pearl Harbor, all thoughts of invading Europe were temporarily shelved in the face of the military exigencies of the Pacific. Political pressures were strong in behalf of concentration on defense of the American coasts as public fears of invasion developed. Several months passed in 1942 before the public was assured that the Japanese were not going to occupy Hawaii and that the West Coast was in no danger of an invasion. Only then was it considered practical to take up once more the planning for the defeat of Germany on the Continent.

General George Marshall secured the approval of the President in April of 1942 for a set of plans dealing with the future confrontation with Hitler's forces. If the Soviet Union appeared in danger of collapse, an emergency invasion was to be attempted in

September of 1942, Operation SLEDGEHAMMER. The full-scale invasion was projected for the spring of 1943, ROUNDUP, a cross-Channel movement that would aim at the heart of the Third Reich. A troop build-up in Britain, Operation BOLERO, was scheduled to bring a million Americans in some 30 divisions to join 18 British divisions to make up an army large enough to land in France. This was far short of the original 800 divisions thought necessary, but the continued Soviet resistance meant that the Germans would be unable to throw their full strength against the Anglo-American armies.

When the spring of 1943 arrived, only a half million Americans had crossed the Atlantic and only about a hundred thousand of these men were in the British Isles; the bulk of the American fighting forces were in combat in North Africa. The troop build-up was 90 percent behind schedule, and no major military planner was optimistic enough to think that a successful landing and beachhead could be established in France with such a drastic cut in strength. "We've got to go to Europe and fight—and we've got to quit wasting resources all over the world—and still worse—wasting time," Dwight Eisenhower, the future commander of the invasion forces, wrote in January of 1942. The failure to act in this fashion and the delay of the cross-Channel attack until June of 1944 had important military effects on the course of the war, effects that in turn shaped the political character of the peace.

Why Allied strategy postponed the reconquest of France and instead engaged in peripheral engagements is a subject over which the historians have debated and will debate for many decades. Many of the factors that produced the delay are clear, but the assumptions behind the decisions to delay are more complex. The issues have also involved national pride so that the debate has not been devoid of the nationalistic biases of the debaters.

There is some measure of agreement that Churchill wanted to avoid a major assault on the shores of France with a massive army as long as possible. At times he appears to have believed that such an operation would very likely not be necessary for victory. If so, the risk of another blood bath was best avoided with German defeat achievable at a much lower price. The Germans, the Prime Minister preached, should be attacked where they were weakest, not where strongest. With this claim he pressed successfully for the North African invasion of November of 1942, an operation that diverted many men and ships from BOLERO. The landings in Sicily and in southern Italy that Churchill supported in 1943 further sapped the build-up for the cross-Channel attack. Opponents of this strategy, chiefly American, condemned it as "periphery-pecking" and "scatterization," since the main task was the traditional route to military victory, the destruction of the main body of the enemy forces by superior strength. Churchill's critics do not estimate, however, what the higher price in British and American lives such a direct strategy would have required even if it had ended the European war six months to a year earlier. They can point out that the saving of lives is, up to a point, not the purpose of the war effort and, once war has begun, a nation's resources are expendable in order to achieve the political ends.

Churchill's supporters and some Americans made another claim for the best means to victory at the lowest cost, the strategic bombing program. One marshal of the Royal Air Force, Lord Trenchard, preached in the intra-war years the concentration of air power on strategic bombing. The most desirable targets, he argued, were the main centers of population, where the effect on human morale would be twenty times as important as the physical destruction inflicted on the enemy. Churchill's chief scientific adviser, F. A. Lindemann, later Lord Cherwell, reinforced this thesis in a memorandum submitted to the Prime Minister in March of 1942. With what seemed an impressive array of scientific data, Lindemann claimed that the bombing of working class districts of fifty-eight large German towns and cities would in eighteen months leave a majority of the population homeless and break the civilian morale to a point where it would be impossible to continue the war. Some scientists saw flaws in Lindemann's assumptions, but he was supported by strategic bombing enthusiasts in the American forces and made a convincing case to the Prime Minister.

The Bomber Command of the Royal Air Force was assigned

this task and by the fall of 1942 began to be aided by the arrival of the American Eighth Air Force. Criticized at times by the regular Army and Navy officers as "bomber barons," the Army Air Force leaders began an operation that they claimed would destroy German resistance. A priority system was established for the destruction of German war industries and their productive capacities were slated to be bombed out of existence. In time, much of Germany and the industrial Ruhr in particular was reduced to rubble, with somewhere between two hundred and six hundred thousand civilians being killed in raids on urban centers.

In perspective, two criticisms can be made of this effort at victory. The first is that the results were far short of what the proponents claimed for strategic bombing. As stated by Noble Frankland, official historian of the R.A.F., "the effects upon the German capacity and will to continue the war were remarkably small." Production of war materials, despite the bombing, continued to rise in volume until it reached a peak in August of 1944. German civilian morale failed to crack as the factory worker suffered the destruction of his city as stoically as British workers did in 1940–41. Only in the spring of 1945, as Germany was invaded from the east and west, did the bombing begin to cripple the warmaking economy. The accuracy of the raids was never close to the claims made, and some important factories survived several reportedly obliterating bombings with only scattered hits.

The second argument against the bombing program has been its effect in delaying the opening of the Second Front. The manufacture of bombing planes had first priority and slowed the production of tactical planes for use in troop support. The Battle of the Atlantic against German U-boats was also hampered by the low priority given to long-range patrol planes, which had proved their effectiveness against this method of German severance of the supply lines from the United States. Commanders of the anti-submarine patrols claim that with an adequate number of planes and pilots they could have drastically cut the merchant marine losses by driving the German undersea fleet from the Atlantic. The flow of men and machines to Britain would then have been great enough to support a much earlier assault on Europe.

Washington, as British writers are likely to point out, made its own contribution to the retardation of D-Day. Before Pearl Harbor it was fully agreed that American strategy was to "Beat Hitler first," and to give top priority to Europe. But once war raged in the Pacific and the area commanders pleaded for more men and ships, it was difficult to refuse immediate Pacific needs in order to prepare for future campaigns in Europe. Fleet Admiral Ernest King was at one point prepared to give the Pacific first priority as long as Britain was not ready to accept the American date for the landings in France. Roosevelt was determined to retain the European priority, but this still did not prevent some siphoning off for the campaigns against Japan of resources that the British felt should be reserved for Europe.

American mobilization in 1942 and 1943 was also far more sluggish than the exigencies of military action permitted. The Selective Service inductions to meet the estimated manpower needs proved more difficult than was expected. A "guns *and* butter" outlook in a major segment of American society checked any political decision to squeeze the economy until serious sacrifices of living standards were required. As a result the Chief of Staff was induced to scale down what had been assumed the essential size of the armed forces. The Victory Program drafted before Pearl Harbor had estimated an eventual peak Army strength of 213 divisions. Throughout 1942 the War Department continued to assume that at least 200 divisions were going to be necessary, although as the demands of the Pacific increased some planners estimated as high as 350 divisions. But a special committee report for the Chief of Staff in April of 1943 warned of the practical limits to the number that could be inducted.

Faced with political limits on military requirements the Army cut its goal back to 100 divisions. But even this level proved too difficult to reach. In early April of 1944, with D-Day only weeks away, General Marshall faced a deficiency of between three and four hundred thousand men. The decision taken, "the 90 division gamble," in the words of Army historian Maurice Matloff, was the greatest calculated risk in the preparations for the invasion of Europe. The gamble succeeded, and the beachhead was established. The risk remained, however, and the manpower estimate again was tested in late 1944 when German forces took the offensive in the Battle of the Bulge. At that point the American reserves were completely exhausted in checking the onrushing *Panzer* army, and almost nothing stood between the German spearhead and the Channel when the thrust ended. It was six weeks before the American forces could resume their drive toward the German frontier. While disaster was avoided, the Roosevelt administration's policy of letting domestic political considerations make such military gambles necessary was a dangerous one.

The political costs of the limited mobilizations and of the delay in establishing a Second Front were lasting ones and immediately relevant to the future of Europe. By the time the Anglo-American forces were established on their Normandy beachhead, the forces of the Soviet Union had driven the Germans out of the Ukraine and had crossed the prewar borders of Poland and Rumania. The *cordon sanitaire* was pierced and would soon be broken.

When the victorious armies under General Eisenhower at last reached the Rhine in March of 1945, the Soviet forces had already crossed the Oder River. Behind them they occupied all of the Baltic states, Poland, Rumania, and a substantial segment of Czechoslovakia and Hungary. Some strategic prizes remained, parts of Czechoslovakia and possibly even Berlin. But American military leaders assumed that their task was to defeat the enemy at minimal cost in lives without regard to the political consequences. When a British suggestion was made that General George Patton drive on to Czechoslovakia and take Prague before the Russians, General Marshall told Eisenhower, "I would be loath to hazard American lives for purely political reasons." Eisenhower replied in the same line of thought, "I shall not attempt any move I deem

militarily unwise merely to gain a political advantage unless I
receive specific orders from the Combined Chiefs of Staff."

Disregard for the political significance of military action also
contributed to the actions by which Germany was divided on a line
that left the capital deep in the zone of Soviet occupation. The
possibility of the capture of Berlin was open to the forces com-
manded by General Eisenhower, but dismissed in order to concentrate on the encirclement and capture of the Ruhr. Berlin would
have been a costly target, but from a political point of view a very
important one. Lives were saved and a stronger strategic position
in central Germany sacrificed.

The decision to postpone the Second Front and to avoid a
frontal attack on the *Wehrmacht* saved many British and American lives. When D-Day came, Germany's Westwall was not
manned by the cream of the Nazi armies, but by divisions in which
old men and boys filled the vacancies created by the tremendous
casualties on the Eastern Front. Britain lost in World War II only
half as many men as fell in France in 1914–18, and only ten
percent of British losses took place in Europe during the eleven
months between D-Day and VE-Day. The United States carried
the heavier manpower responsibilities, but the 130,000 Americans
who died in combat in Europe were still less than four percent of
the approximately 2.8 million Germans who died before the
German Reich collapsed.

MILITARY LOSSES IN WORLD WAR II

U.S.S.R.	7.5 million or 1 out of 22 of 1940 population
Germany	2.8 million or 1 out of 25 of 1940 population
Japan	1.5 million or 1 out of 46 of 1940 population
G.B.	300 thousand or 1 out of 150 of 1940 population
U.S.A.	290 thousand or 1 out of 500 of 1940 population
France	200 thousand or 1 out of 200 of 1940 population

British and American strategy left to the Soviet Union the
chief task of killing Germans for approximately three years.
During that period the Red Army engaged about 180 German

divisions while the British and American forces in North Africa and Italy tied down less than 10 German divisions. Of the almost three million Germans believed to have died in combat, over 85 percent were killed on the Eastern Front. To accomplish this, despite initial technical inferiority, the Soviet Union, according to American estimates, sacrificed 7.5 million men who checked and finally drove the German forces back into Central Europe. Even without the additional millions of Russians who died of cold, disease, and malnutrition, this was the greatest price paid by any nation in any war. Estimates of civilian losses customarily are greater than those of combat, bringing the total Soviet deaths to well over 15 million.

For Britain, France, and the United States the military objective of destroying German armed strength was accomplished at a minimal cost. The Lend-Lease food and the Lend-Lease arms put into the hands of the Russians were a small financial price to pay for the efforts of a hard-fighting ally. But the political price was a victorious Soviet Union which saw itself as carrying the major burden of the war and which found itself on VE-Day in occupation of all of Eastern and much of Central Europe. Hardened by the long years of combat and sacrifice, the leaders of the Kremlin were understandably cold to the claims that the boundaries and politics of the areas they occupied should be settled in close cooperation with allies they felt had contributed so much less to victory.

6

A Strained and Strange Alliance

Writing at the close of the eighteenth century and viewing its many coalition wars, the Comte de Ségur concluded that alliances are "marriages followed promptly by divorce." Although an interest in defeating a common enemy "momentarily unites, a constant jealousy separates." The linkage between Washington, London, and Moscow could not escape this generalization no matter how frequent the professions of amity and unity. Each was fighting a war for different ends from a background of divers and conflicting interests.

Churchill was always aware of his incompatibilities with his allies because of his absorption of his country's historic policies and its responsibilities of empire. Roosevelt was less conscious of the unavoidable contradictions of interests in the coalition, particularly in respect to American relations with Britain. Common Anglo-American ideals seemed adequate to him for covering over the divergencies with London. It was the Russians who were most sensitive to the possibility that the defeat of Hitler would again find Western Europe aligned against the Eastern center of power.

Ideology accounts for only a part of the distrust with which the Kremlin viewed the Anglo-American Front. Historic experiences alone were enough to account for all of the suspicion that

Stalin and his aides retained for Soviet allies. Even the military progress of the war was often a guarded secret. The American Lend-Lease staff in Moscow, providing where possible for the needs of the Red Army, were still given few glimpses of the military operations. It was "a strange alliance," Major General John Deane concluded on the basis of his experience as military attaché in Moscow during the war years.

The Russians were often explicit in stating their views of their interests and gave fair warning to the Allies of the issues over which there was likely to be conflict. After Eden's mission to Moscow in December of 1941, the British Foreign Office knew the nature of Soviet ambitions in Eastern Europe and recognized that the limitations of British power would require many compromises on their part. It was Roosevelt, Hull, and some of the White House advisers who were slow to see that the Russians were serious about protecting and advancing their historic goals and ambitions.

President Roosevelt's attitude toward the Soviet Union and Soviet Communism has been subject to extreme partisan interpretations helped by the sparseness of the record of his thoughts. In February of 1940 he talked about Communism to the American Youth Congress, an audience that included a number of Communist Party members and sympathizers. In the early days of the Russian Revolution, Roosevelt said, he had had great sympathy for the people of that nation and recognized that the new leaders were bringing education, better health, and better opportunities for the masses. But he "disliked the regimentation," "abhorred the indiscriminate killing," and "heartily deprecated the banishment of religion." He hoped that the Soviet Union would eventually become "a peace-loving, popular government with a free ballot which would not interfere with the integrity of its neighbors." That early hope, Roosevelt said in 1940, was either shattered or had to be "put away in storage against some better day."

Like many Americans, Roosevelt began to look more favorably on the Soviet Union when it bore up under the weight of the German attack. In the first week of the Russo-German War,

Roosevelt told Admiral Leahy that if this clash were more than a diversion, it might mean the liberation of Europe from Nazi domination. "At the same time I do not think we need worry about any possibility of Russian domination," said the President. If Roosevelt changed his mind in this respect, it was not until the spring of 1945. In 1944 Secretary of Treasury Morgenthau told him that there were two kinds of people. One was like Anthony Eden, who believed "that we must co-operate with the Russians and that we must trust Russia for the peace of the world." The other kind was exemplified by Churchill, whose fear of the Soviet Union led him to ask, "What are we going to have between the white snows of Russia and the white cliffs of Dover?" Roosevelt said that Morgenthau had stated the matter well; "I belong to the same school as Eden."

Efforts to raise Roosevelt's doubts over the viability of the Russian-American relationship, sometimes made for purposes of political harassment, were met with great presidential self-assurance. The decision in November of 1941 to extend Lend-Lease to the Soviet Union was a bold one which drew many attacks. In a press conference in February of 1942 the President was asked whether it was not dangerous to make loans to Russia if they were going to become powerful after the war. He dismissed the question as an argument coming from what he called "the Cliveden set of Washington," a reference to Britain's prewar appeasers. When asked to comment on the value of military aid to Russia, Roosevelt said, "Put it in terms of dead Germans and smashed tanks." Roosevelt never failed to recognize the crucial importance of the Soviet military effort. "Whether we win or lose the war depends on the Russians," he told Morgenthau in June of 1942. If the Russians could keep three and a half million Germans engaged throughout the summer, he said, "we can definitely win." The President felt that the British had let the Russians down in respect to promised military aid, and he was determined that the United States not lag in meeting Lend-Lease schedules. "I would go out and take the stuff off the shelves of the stores and pay them any price necessary and put it in a truck and rush it to the boat," he said in March of 1942. No military disaster could then be worse, as he saw it, than a Russian collapse, even the loss of New Zealand and Australia to Japan.

The President's appreciation of the military contribution of the Soviet Union in time found some support in public opinion. The hostility towards Bolshevism and Red Russia that developed in the 1920's and 1930's was still widespread at the time of Hitler's attack and had been intensified by Russia's attack on Finland. The mass media, encouraged by Washington and in line with patriotic calls for support of Allied unity, began changing the existing stereotypes. Already in September of 1941 the readers of the mass circulation magazine *Life* were given a new image of Stalin: "Whatever the politics of this stocky little dictator, he is the man who has so far come nearest to stopping the German Wehrmacht." One of the leading American female photographers presented a close-up of Stalin in the same issue along with her impression of him, "a great deal of charm and a magnetic personality." In March of 1943, when this same publication devoted almost an entire issue to the Soviet Union, Russians were described as "one hell of a people" who "look like Americans, dress like Americans and think like Americans."

The dark spots in the Soviet Union were viewed in a new light. The notorious Russian secret police, the NKVD, were described in *Life* as "a national police similar to the F.B.I." whose job was "tracking down traitors." Americans were reminded that the Soviet Union was once "the greatest advocate of collective security" but had learned, after Munich, to play a lone hand. It was possible, Americans were warned, that the Soviet Union might do this in the future, annexing strategic areas in the name of security. To prevent this, *Life,* along with many other editorialists and radio commentators, urged that Russia be made to realize the friendship of the United States and that Americans were willing to enter into a strong security system at the end of the war.

Books as well as magazines disseminated an optimistic view of the Russian-American relationship, present and future, in the interest of maintaining a high wartime morale. One of the widest-read proponents of this view was former Ambassador Joseph Davies, whose book *Mission to Moscow* became a leading nonfiction best seller in 1942 and continued to sell well in subsequent years. It worked on such an expedient theme that a motion picture was produced from the book, using the same title. Davies said nothing about the Soviet Union to offend the most ardent Russophile. Maxim Litvinov was quoted by the publisher's advertisements as saying that it presented the facts with "the utmost precision and truthfulness" while the Communist *Daily Worker* praised the volume for its "realistic, clear-cut and objective reporting."

A number of national polls indicated that the new view of the Soviet Union, possibly as one-sided as the old, was having its effect. The frequent headlines announcing Soviet victories when there was no great news of British or American action began to convince the public that Russians were brave and patriotic people whose political system worked well enough to provide the arms for success. Asked in 1942 which nation they would rather see in control of Europe, Germany or Russia, 71 percent of the pollees answered Russia, only 6 percent favored Germany, and 23 percent confessed that they did not know. A *Fortune* magazine poll in 1943 found that business executives had more confidence in Russian good intentions than the average American. Some 48 percent of the executives believed that after the war the Soviet Union would not try to bring about Communist governments in other countries while only 31 percent of the general public polled held the same belief. As late as January of 1945 the optimism was still strong. Asked, "Do you think we shall get along better with Russia in the future than we did in the past, not so well or about the same?" more than twice as many Americans saw improved relations in the future as expected deterioration.

Not all Americans in the Roosevelt administration were optimistic about reaching satisfactory agreements with Moscow or unqualifiedly in support of the effort to establish a close partnership. A State Department memorandum for the British Foreign Office, a week before the German invasion, stated American policy

as opposing new approaches to the Soviet Union and treating with
reserve any Soviet approaches. The Department intended to reject
any suggestions from Moscow for concessions in the interest of
better relations and "to exact a strict *quid pro quo* for anything we
are willing to give the Soviet Union." Even the expected outbreak
of war between Russia and Germany should not, some believed,
change this American position. A memorandum prepared by the
Division of European Affairs, dated June 21, 1941, urged that the
United States should "steadfastedly adhere to the line that the fact
that the Soviet Union is fighting Germany does not mean that it is
defending, struggling for, or adhering to, the principles in international relations which we are supporting."

This caution proved difficult, if not impossible, to retain.
Democracies cannot fight wars with enthusiasm and a willingness
to sacrifice while viewing a major ally with coolness and suspicion
as a potential future enemy. But *not* to hold to that wise detachment was certain, as some foresaw, to create trouble. Secretary of
the Navy Frank Knox glimpsed this when he wrote to his wife in
May of 1942 about the commutation of the prison sentence of Earl
Browder, head of the American Communist Party. This action was
taken, he said, because "our own interests dictate we shall suppress
a disposition to denounce communism in behalf of national security." At the same time Knox wrote, "I hate to think of the
unholy mess that awaits the assembling of the peace delegates
when peace comes if Russia is still an ally."

Between the hard-liners as represented by some elements in
the State Department and the soft-liners as represented in 1942
and 1943 by the White House, there seem to have been few who
took a middle ground. That position was sketched by an editorial
writer, in the popular weekly *Collier's* in April of 1943, who wrote
that Americans should:

> Look at Russia as we look at any other nation fighting on our
> side. Expect Russia to think of itself first and last, and to get any
> added power and territory out of this war it can. Don't idealize
> Russia, don't consider it a devil-nation either; just view it as a

huge collection of human beings who will act in any situation as other human beings will act.

Although a decade later the majority of Americans would probably have judged the devil-nation theory the valid one, this was in part the creation of those who too long denied the existence of Russian national interests and expected a victorious nation not to demand rewards for the blood its people had shed in its defense. There was no Atlantic between the Russians and Germany, not even a Channel, as Anthony Eden said in retrospect, and it would have been feckless of any Russian government not to take precautions for its future security. No revival of the Wilsonian dream of a Europe devoid of conflicts of power and prestige, fully secure in some new form of international organization, was likely to be strong enough to convince any Russian ruler to accept a return to the prewar *status quo* on the Eastern European frontier.

Roosevelt's failure to foresee the continued role of balance of power politics in Europe has been the basis for much of the criticism of the decisions of the Casablanca Conference of January 14–24, 1943. The initiative for this fourth meeting between Roosevelt and Churchill came from the President, who hoped that it would be the first meeting of the Big Three. Roosevelt and Churchill had few difficulties in arranging their conferences. Both men liked to break their regular routines, and Churchill seems to have enjoyed the opportunity to escape the strains of wartime London in a warmer climate and less intense atmosphere. Roosevelt's inclination to go overseas was checked by political considerations. Wilson's trips to Paris in 1919 were his chief precedent and one that carried a weight of unpleasant associations. The engagement of American troops in North Africa finally provided public justification for a trip to that area. The President's mood at Casablanca, according to one observer, Robert Murphy, was that of "a schoolboy on vacation." Churchill responded similarly to the delights of the Moroccan climate and scenery, and on a pleasurable side trip to Marrakech, the capital of the sultanate, turned to his easel and painted for the first time since the outbreak of the war.

Roosevelt invited Stalin in November of 1942 and again in December. He said that the compelling reason for conferring was that "I am very anxious to have a talk with you." Stalin rejected both offers by saying that he could not leave his direction of the war and that pressing matters could be handled by correspondence. Churchill was not anxious for a meeting with the Russian premier, whom he had seen in August of 1942, and felt that it would center on the embarrassing question of the Second Front.

Most of the Casablanca conference was devoted to military matters: the question of the strategy to be followed after the imminent victory over the Axis forces in North Africa. A decision was made to invade Sicily, Operation HUSKY. Stalin was informed of agreement on "large-scale amphibious operations in the Mediterranean" while other forces were being concentrated in Britain to prepare to re-enter the continent of Europe "as soon as practicable." Anglo-American operations in the first nine months of 1943, along with Russian action "may well bring Germany to her knees in 1943," according to the joint cable to the Russian premier. Stalin replied, stating that he assumed that the decisions on Germany were designed to open up the front in 1943 and asking for information on concrete operations planned. Churchill framed an answer that said that preparations were being pushed "to the limit of our resources" for a cross-Channel operation in August. If the operation was delayed by weather or other reasons, "it will be prepared with stronger forces for September." Stalin still did not like the late summer date, preferring a spring operation, and claiming that the Germans had since December moved some 27 divisions from France and the West to join in the battle against Russia.

On the last day of the Conference, January 24, the President issued a statement to the press in which he said:

> Peace can come to the world only by the total elimination of German and Japanese war power. . . . The elimination of German, Japanese and Italian war power means the unconditional surrender by Germany, Italy and Japan. That means a reason-

able assurance of future world peace. It does not mean the destruction of the population of Germany, Italy or Japan, but it does mean the destruction of the philosophies in those countries which are based on conquest and the subjugation of other people.

The phrase "unconditional surrender" Roosevelt later said, had just "popped" into his mind and he associated it, mistakenly, with Grant's dealings with Lee at Appomattox. (Grant had not used the term with Lee, but with General Buckner in the surrender of Fort Donelson three years earlier.) Churchill for a time supported Roosevelt's story on the impromptu origins of this famous term, but discovered in writing his memoirs that he had consulted the cabinet on the use of the phrase four days earlier. The phrase had also been used by a State Department Subcommittee on Security Problems and reported to Roosevelt, along with a recommendation of the Joint Chiefs of Staff in December of 1942 that no armistice be granted any of the enemies until they accepted unconditional surrender of their armed forces.

One of the strongest critics of the new policy was Secretary of State Hull. The President had not taken him to North Africa, asking Churchill to leave Eden home as well. The Secretary claimed that this principle had not formed part of the State Department's thinking and opposed it for two reasons. The first was that unconditional surrender might provoke a desperation, despite the qualifying terms, that would solidify Axis resistance and prolong the war. Hitler's Minister of Propaganda Joseph Goebbels did use the phrase in his efforts to strengthen German morale. Hull also felt that total victory logically required a readiness to take over completely the functions of the defeated governments, nationally and locally, an obligation for which there was little preparation. Others argued that the term "unconditional surrender" abetted the complete destruction of German power, thus creating the political vacuum that later seemed so favorable to the extension of Russian power. The validity of this approach to the enemy depended for the most part on the kind of postwar world to be created. In Roosevelt's completely disarmed international society, run by the Four Policemen, Germany would have no military power and to permit the *Wehrmacht* to remain intact in surrender would have created additional obstacles for the policemen. But if, as at the end of the Napoleonic wars, the coalition was to realign itself into rival blocs, Germany was likely to lean towards the West and its strength would be a valuable asset.

Such theoretical considerations assume what was not likely to be true, that public morale could be maintained in Britain and the United States in an obviously limited war, and that men would willingly die for a goal short of total victory over the enemy. A total war that almost fully engages the energies of a society creates strong political demands for total victory. Woodrow Wilson's aspiration for "a peace without victory" had not been made to a nation with over thirteen million men under arms, as in 1943, and even Wilson had been countered by the formation of "Unconditional Surrender Clubs" throughout the country by his Republican opponents. One war later there were many more Americans who felt that *this time* the Germans must be defeated completely and without mercy. Roosevelt's "unconditional surrender" phrase was to a great extent an expression of popular will, whatever folly it may have been as a technique for recreating a stable Europe favorable to Anglo-American interests and ideals.

The outlines of that future Europe still remained very hazy after Casablanca. Churchill constantly produced new ideas for fighting the war, but his mind, as Field Marshal Jan Smuts told Eden, "had a stop in it at the end of the war." Eden was far more concerned about the specifics of the future settlement and came to Washington in mid-March of 1943 to talk to the President and State Department officials. Eden brought with him a statement of Soviet aspirations to be considered in Anglo-American planning. The resulting discussions were the fullest and most detailed of any held up to that point.

A central issue to be settled was the future of Germany, and Eden pressed for some guidelines. He did not think that Stalin wanted to take full responsibility for Germany, but still hoped to have Anglo-American forces on German soil when the Nazi regime collapsed so that the task of occupation could be shared. Eden also felt that Stalin would insist on the breakup of the Reich into a number of smaller states to prevent any future German threat. Roosevelt in March of 1943 did not oppose a division of Germany, but hoped, unrealistically, that it would be the product of indigenous separatist movements and not have to be imposed by the victors. When Eden asked what Roosevelt favored doing if no separatism developed, the President said that he favored a division of Germany under any circumstances. Prussia, in particular, he said, must be made a separate state. Stalin and Roosevelt therefore seemed in basic agreement. Only Ambassador Halifax at this conference pointed to the dynamics of German nationalism and suggested that a forced division might provide the sort of major grievance that could produce a new Hitler. Halifax urged that consideration be given to decentralization rather than partition, using some form of United Nations control to maintain demilitarization.

The conferees in Washington spent considerable time on Eastern Europe and the question of the postwar borders of the Soviet Union. As Eden reported, the Russians were demanding the frontier with Finland established after victory in 1940, providing a buffer area for Leningrad. The Russians also wanted the Finnish seaport of Hango at the entrance to the Gulf of Finland, a concession made in the 1940 peace. Soviet power was to be further extended in Scandinavia by a "mutual assistance pact" that would give the Soviet Union access to Finnish air bases. Eden and Roosevelt both thought that the 1940 frontier was a reasonable request, but that the Russians should make concessions to the Finns by modifying their additional demands. The alternatives were not stated, and Eden and Roosevelt agreed that the postwar settlement with Finland would be difficult to arrange on lines they considered most desirable.

On the southern coast of the Baltic, Eden reported that the Soviet Union was adamant in respect to the incorporation of Latvia, Lithuania, and Estonia and would not reconsider the 1940 action. The security interest provided the chief justification for

Moscow's claim to this area although a historic argument could be made as well for regaining Tsarist territories. But the Russians also claimed popular support for annexation in the three small countries on the basis of a very questionable plebiscite in 1939. Roosevelt recognized that annexation could not be prevented; a new plebiscite ought to be urged on the Russians nevertheless. He was also unwilling to recognize what the Red Army would soon make a *fait accompli,* and believed that this nonrecognition might be a means of extracting Soviet concessions elsewhere.

The largest Eastern European state posed even greater problems. The Polish issue was not only historically complex, but it involved many irrational elements, creating the most troublesome question in Russo-American relations. When the Polish Army collapsed in the fall of 1939, members of the Polish government fled to France via Rumania and formed a government in exile. Recognized by both Britain and the United States, the Poles moved their government to London with the fall of France. As refugees their life was a difficult one, perhaps accentuating the exasperating extremes of their nationalism. Although they were supported by financial contributions from Britain and the United States, this relationship did not prevent the Poles from periodically embarrassing their hosts with vigorous expressions of hostility towards Russia.

Polish animosity towards Russia had a long history. The nationalistic Polish leaders could not forget the glories of the fifteenth and sixteenth centuries when their empire extended deep into the territory of modern Russia, embracing the Ukraine and at one point pressing the shores of the Black Sea. More than a century of nonexistence as a state after the final partition of 1795 had not extinguished the dreams of greatness. The so-called Curzon line drafted for the eastern Polish frontier had been viewed as "a British sword of Damocles" and quite unacceptable. Victory over the Russians in 1921 had pushed the boundary further eastward and given the Poles a zone of over ten million people of whom little more than a third were Polish. No Polish government was subsequently willing to negotiate major changes of this boundary;

some nationalists pointed out that another million Poles still lived to the east of that boundary, scattered among Slavic peoples. The development of the Soviet Union as a major power and the crushing defeat suffered by Poland in 1939 did not produce any willingness to adjust boundaries to the new political conditions.

The Russians reciprocated Polish animosity and showed contempt for a government that had boasted in 1939 of its ability to defend itself without Soviet aid. The units of the Polish Army that surrendered to the Russians were treated roughly, and many were sent to labor camps under extreme conditions. Several thousand Polish officers were, for reasons that remain obscure, shot and buried in a mass grave in the forest of Katyn near Smolensk. Although the weight of the evidence points to Russian guilt, Moscow put the blame on the Germans with claims that never convinced the London Poles. While the Katyn affair produced considerable heat, the insuperable barrier between Moscow and the government in exile was the boundary that the Soviet Union regained in 1939.

In the interests of wartime unity the British government had promoted the establishment of diplomatic relations between Moscow and the Polish government in exile in July of 1941. The exchanges remained very cool and, on occasion, Polish "demands" were made on the Soviet Union that may have had some justification but that were hardly consonant with the position of a powerless body, living as the guests of a Soviet ally. When the London government pressed for a Red Cross investigation of the Katyn murders, the Soviet Union used the occasion to break relations with the exiles headed by General Sikorski. In Poland itself a London-supported underground competed with and fought against a Russian-aided underground, both claiming to represent the Polish people in the struggle against the Nazi occupation forces.

The United States not only recognized the London Poles, but included that government in the Lend-Lease program. The Poles, in turn, looked to Roosevelt as their defender and flooded the State Department with their grievances, pleading for action in their behalf against the Soviet Union. Repeatedly the President did ask

American representatives to intercede in Moscow, with little result.

The willingness of the President to accept the extreme and at times irritating behavior of this exile group was in good part explained by the Polish-American vote and the votes of other ethnic blocs that were Eastern European in origin and that followed the fate of the Poles with interest. But there may have also have been some romantic feeling in Washington for these ardent nationalists, similar to that which stirred England in the 1830's and which influenced Woodrow Wilson in World War I. In any case, Roosevelt was far more willing than Churchill or Eden to issue amorphous statements in support of the Polish state from which the exiles were able to maintain a faith that the United States would eventually stand between them and their Russian neighbor.

Eden reported to Roosevelt in March of 1943 his difficulties with the Polish representatives who had such large postwar ambitions, hoping that Germany would be crushed and Russia so weakened that Poland would be the strongest state in that part of the world. The President agreed that this was unrealistic and that the Poles would have to accept the decisions of the Big Three. He also was willing, as was Eden, to give East Prussia to the Poles, moving the German population out; even if this was a harsh procedure, it was one that would contribute to maintaining the peace. Eden said that the Russians also privately agreed on ceding East Prussia, but were unwilling to tell the Poles until the final boundary discussion. Stalin wanted a strong Poland, Eden believed, providing the right people were running it; Roosevelt felt this would be a difficult basis on which to consider boundaries since a "liberal government" at the time of the Peace Conference might well be thrown out in a year.

For the rest of Eastern Europe Stalin favored the restoration of the 1938 boundaries with the exception of the restoration of Bessarabia to Russian rule. Rumania might be compensated with some Hungarian territory since Stalin felt the Hungarians should be punished. None of the other Eastern European or Balkan questions seemed to pose serious difficulties. Roosevelt did feel that Yugoslavia should not be preserved since he claimed that Croats and Serbs ought not to be forced to live together. Serbia he favored as an independent state with the Croats put under an international trusteeship. Eden disagreed, viewing Yugoslavia as a viable state.

The British favored the creation of two federations, one composed of Balkan states, the other of Eastern European states to the north. The Polish government in exile also supported federation, wanting one large organization embracing all the states south to Turkey. But as Sumner Welles warned General Sikorski in January of 1943, the Russians would suspect that this was a new version of the *cordon sanitaire*. Stalin had the reverse in mind, as Ambassador Standley suggested, writing from Moscow in April of 1943:

> It has occurred to me that we may be faced with a turn-about in European history. In 1918 Western Europe attempted to set up a *cordon sanitaire* to protect it from the influence of bolshevism. Might not now the Kremlin envisage the formation of a belt of pro-Soviet states to protect it from the influences of the West?

Roosevelt may not have given any consideration to the Ambassador's warning, but he did not respond to the federation concept. Any security problems in this area, he believed, should be handled by the Big Three.

Discussing with Eden the composition of the future international organization, Roosevelt again advocated China as a member of the Big Four. Madame Chiang Kai-shek had recently been a White House guest and with charm and vigor pleaded China's cause. The British were skeptical in respect to China's great power claims. Roosevelt argued the need for Chinese manpower in policing Japan, and in any serious conflict with the Russians, he assured Eden that the Chinese would undoubtedly line up with Britain and the United States. This was one of the few instances in which the President took note that his Four Policemen might have some serious disagreements with the Soviet Union, which was apparently to be in a minority of one. Below the Four Policemen, as

Roosevelt sketched it for Eden, was to be a general assembly in which all nations would be represented, but it would meet only about once a year and its purpose would be to enable the smaller powers "to blow off steam." An advisory council, consisting of the Big Four and six to eight smaller powers, elected on a regional basis, would be used to settle any international questions while the Big Four alone wielded police power.

The issue on which the White House and the British Foreign Office found themselves farthest apart was the American program for the liquidation of colonialism. Roosevelt was prepared not only to strip Japan of its colonies in Asia but to do the same for France, Britain, and Portugal. (No mention of the Dutch East Indies other than Timor was noted in the record.) These areas would then be held in trusteeship by the Big Four until ready for independence. Eden was cool to the trusteeship idea, particularly since the President several times mentioned Hong Kong. Some strategic bases, Roosevelt said, should be held by the Big Four, each furnishing troops for specific bases. The President thought that the United States could furnish troops for a Formosan base and also for Dakar in French Senegal. Roosevelt did not speak of the political obstacles to such a major change of international society, and Eden made little comment.

In another area the two conferring parties reached little agreement; this was the question of the Free French authorities and General de Gaulle. The United States recognized the Vichy Government until the Germans completely overran France in November of 1942. Churchill had refused to deal with the Vichy regime and instead saw Charles de Gaulle as the future French leader. But the leader of the Free French was viewed skeptically by both Roosevelt and Hull. The differences went even deeper than the personality of the proud General; Britain still viewed France as a major factor in future European politics and as a neighbor whose interests were to be defended. Roosevelt still assumed in 1943 that France would be a power of negligible importance and was prepared to completely disarm that nation and strip it of its overseas colonies.

Returning to London, Anthony Eden noted that the President's quick opinions on very complex issues were alarming for their "cheerful fecklessness." Without much consideration of the political and historical factors involved, Roosevelt appeared ready to make quick decisions that disposed of the fate of many lands. The British had little of the American optimism about the ease with which a new world could be made. The British Foreign Office also recognized that their Russian ally had strong convictions about national security needs and had yet to be converted to the views of the White House.

7

Quebec, Moscow, and Teheran: 1943

The fourth year of the European War and the second year of American participation was a period of frequent conferences among the Allies. In addition to Casablanca in January and Eden's trip to Washington in March, Churchill crossed the Atlantic twice to talk with Roosevelt. The Prime Minister first came to Washington in May for a meeting code-named TRIDENT and to Quebec in August for a conference called QUADRANT. The three foreign ministers then met in Moscow in October, planning the first meeting of Roosevelt, Stalin, and Churchill, which finally took place in Persia in November of 1943.

The Roosevelt-Churchill conferences devoted a good deal of time to military operations and to political decisions involving Italy. After control of North Africa was regained, more slowly than expected, Churchill successfully urged another Mediterranean operation, the invasion of Sicily in July of 1943. Shortly after this operation began, Benito Mussolini was deposed, and an Italian government headed by Marshal Pietro Badoglio began to talk of peace. British and American forces then landed in southern Italy in early September, and the Badoglio government quickly surrendered and became a cobelligerent by declaring war on Germany. Hitler's forces in the meantime seized Rome and with reinforcements soon established well-defended lines across the Italian peninsula that kept the Allies south of Rome until June of 1944.

The Russians were cool to the Italian campaigns, seeing this area as one of minor importance and as delaying the opening of the Second Front without drawing off a substantial amount of German strength. Stalin sent his congratulations, however, on the Italian surrender and agreed to its terms. Theoretically the surrender was "unconditional," but in practice it included a number of qualifications in the interest of securing Italian co-operation.

The Russians were also interested in playing a part in the decisions made in respect to Italy's future. Although this request was in line with the repeated American claims that all matters affecting postwar Europe should be a matter of common concern by the Big Three, Roosevelt was determined that Italy would remain in the hands of the Control Commission consisting of British and American representatives. A gesture of co-operation was made in giving the Russians a post on the Allied Advisory Council along with France, and later Greece and Yugoslavia. The Council was given no real authority; it could only make recommendations and was originally established outside of Italy itself in Algeria. The Russians soon recognized the realities of the situation, which provided them with a precedent and device for later exclusion of Britain and the United States from any significant role in Eastern Europe.

At the Quebec Conference in August an attempt was made to settle the difficult issue of France. Eden tried to convince Secretary Hull of the importance of recognizing the Committee of National Liberation led by General de Gaulle, but concluded that Hull had "an obsession against the Free French which nothing can cure." Roosevelt had reacted adversely to the French leader in his brief encounter with him at Casablanca, charging him with a "Jeanne d'Arc complex." The White House and the State Department began a vendetta against the person of the Free French leader that became increasingly difficult for the British as they saw de Gaulle winning wider recognition as the national leader both in and outside of France. Roosevelt at the same time found fewer and fewer non-Gaullist Frenchmen with whom he could deal.

The President's method of handling this incompatibility was

to try to dismiss France completely as an important political factor in the future of Europe. With little success he tried to convince London that Frenchmen looked more to him to protect their interests than to de Gaulle and that France must be treated as a very minor power. But, as Eden reminded Hull, the British lived only twenty miles away from France, and they could not envision a disarmed country, living passively under a regime created by Americans.

Soviet recognition of the Committee of National Liberation in August of 1943 as "the representative of the State interests of the French Republic" further weakened the American position. Efforts to reach agreement between London and Washington failed, and there was still no common policy when the first Anglo-American forces landed on French soil in the summer of 1944.

Eden again tried at Quebec to elucidate the American position in respect to the Soviet Union's boundary claims. Moscow still had no hint, he told Hull, of Washington's stand. If the issue remained open until the Red Army occupied Eastern Europe, he warned, the situation would be difficult to cope with diplomatically. Hull stood with the President in trying to continue to postpone the clash of views until later. All that was agreed on was that if concessions to the Soviet Union were necessary, the United States and Britain must be ready to insist on some form of *quid pro quo*.

Stalin continued to defer a Big Three meeting, despite Roosevelt's appeals, but he did agree in the late summer of 1943 to a conference of the foreign ministers of the three states. As in the case of the proposed locations for the leaders' meeting, he refused to accept a site outside of the Soviet Union and proposed Moscow. Roosevelt favored Moscow over London, still fearing that latent American anglophobia would be aroused by a major conference in the British capital. This stirred British nationalism, and in view of the number of times the British came to Washington, Eden found the President's position "almost insulting."

The skirmishing over the agenda revealed the gap in interests and priorities between the three nations. The Russian draft agenda

began with "measures for shortening the war," a device for pressing the long-awaited invasion of France. The State Department's
draft began with a Four Power statement on general security by
which Hull hoped to tie the Soviet Union to a set of principles on
which postwar co-operation would be based. Eden's proposed
agenda dealt with specific political problems, beginning with the
situation in Italy and the Balkans and including the thorny question of Soviet-Polish relations.

Before Hull left Washington in October for Moscow the
President outlined his views at a White House conference. He
agreed with the priority given to the statement of principles and
insisted on the inclusion of China as a signatory "even at the cost
of getting no agreement at this time." He expected trouble from
the British on this point since "Churchill does not like China."
The Russians with a neutrality pact with Japan were also expected
to oppose formal inclusion of the Chinese government. But Roosevelt was firm in his conviction that the Chinese under Chiang Kai-
shek were going to achieve great power status and deserved a
charter membership in the world police force.

In respect to Germany, Roosevelt still favored partition into
three or more states, all deprived of armed forces and arms industries. He also stated his view that reparations should be taken, not
in money, but in equipment and manpower. This inclusion of
human labor as a form of payment had no precedents in modern
history and later appeared to some of its critics as a throwback to
earlier concepts of vengeance.

The President asked Hull to postpone discussion of the Baltic
states and Poland, matters that he planned to take up directly with
Stalin. On that occasion Roosevelt said that he intended to appeal
to the Soviet leader "on grounds of high morality." The President
knew that appeals on this basis were seldom effective in domestic
politics; to expect such an approach to influence the Soviet Union
was even more difficult to defend. But, Roosevelt said, he was
going to assure the Russians that neither Britain nor the United
States would go to war over the Baltic states while convincing
Russia that it was in their interest to promise a plebiscite to the

peoples of this area within two or more years after the war. It should be of a nature, he believed, that would convince world opinion of its legitimacy as an expression of popular will. The same free choice should be offered to the disputed areas of eastern Poland. In any instance, that border should not give the Russians any more land than offered by the old Curzon line. Lvov, which Roosevelt called by its German name of Lemberg, should go to Poland.

American proposals on trusteeships were to be expanded to include not only colonies in Asia, but also key areas in Europe and the Middle East. Passages to the Baltic, including the Kiel Canal, and an area giving the Russians access to the Persian Gulf were also suggested. How the sovereign states of Denmark, Sweden, and Iran were to be moved to relinquish control in the interests of world peace was not discussed. Nor was mention made of trusteeship for two world waterways of even greater importance, the Suez and Panama canals.

At the age of seventy-two, suffering from claustrophobia and never having previously flown, Cordell Hull arrived in Moscow by air to open the Foreign Ministers' Conference on October 18. His health raised the first question of protocol when he reacted to the chill of Russian fall by attending the first meeting in his overcoat. The hosts tried to be helpful by raising the room temperature to a point at which the British Foreign Minister thought he would faint. A compromise temperature, probably suitable to neither, was agreed upon.

Molotov, chosen as chairman, compiled an agenda, including all items on the three drafts except the American Four Power Declaration, which he felt had no place at a three-power conference. When Hull protested that this was the primary matter on his agenda, Molotov agreed to make it the second item of business, following the primary Russian proposal. As the long agenda was taken up over two weeks, the strongly conflicting national interests of the three powers came to the surface. Each argued for or against certain terms or sought language vague enough to give considerable freedom of interpretation.

For the Russians, facing the third winter of the war with the Germans still holding a line from the outskirts of Leningrad to Kiev and deep into the Ukraine, drastic blows against German power were of greater importance than postwar plans. The first item, "measures to shorten the duration of the war," consisted of a three-point Russian proposal. An Anglo-American pledge to invade France, as planned, in the spring of 1944, headed the list. The British and Americans assured Molotov that Roosevelt and Churchill, meeting at Quebec in August, had reaffirmed their intention to invade, but that no guarantee was possible. Military aides were brought in to discuss the invasion planning, but also to point out that certain preconditions would be required. The strength of the German fighter plane squadrons would have to be reduced, the number of German reserve divisions in the West should be no greater than twelve, and the difficulty of supplying the invaders despite bombed-out ports must be overcome. Some reassurance of Anglo-American intention was all that the Russians could be given.

The second and third Russian points called for three-power representations to bring Turkey immediately into the war against Germany and to secure air bases from Sweden. Any diversion of German strength would be immediately helpful, and to achieve that end Molotov was ready for a collective ultimatum to the two neutrals. The British and Americans backed away from both actions, claiming that the Swedish bases were not needed and that Turkey, although receiving American arms aid, was not ready to enter the war. The Russians considered their allies overly solicitous towards these neutrals and were "unquestionably chagrined" at this attitude, as Ambassador Harriman wrote the President: "The Russians have the primitive view that they have suffered and bled to destroy Hitler and see no reason why the Turks should not do the same if it can help shorten the war." Some minor satisfaction was given the Russians by an agreement with Britain, later joined by the United States, to suggest to Turkey entry into the war before the end of 1943 and in the meantime to make available air bases for the Allies. But when the Turks were approached by Eden in early November of 1943, they flatly refused to make concessions.

Italy also continued to be an area in which the Russians received little satisfaction. The Italian Navy had surrendered, and the merchant marine was being transferred to British and American control; the Soviet Union held that it should be given approximately one-third share in these spoils of war. Churchill agreed in principle, but wanted the two Italian battleships assigned to Britain because of the Royal Navy's losses in that category of ships. Roosevelt was initially against any sharing, supported by the argument of his Chiefs of Staff who pointed to the adverse effect on Italian public opinion that any cession of ships to the Soviet Union would produce. Seeking the maximum Italian co-operation in continuing the war on the peninsula against the Germans, the military chiefs argued only from expediency.

When Roosevelt later learned how strongly the Russians felt about the division of the Italian naval forces, he agreed to their use of some ships while postponing their final disposition until the peace conference. But concern for Italian reactions, as well as the difficulty of transfer from the Mediterranean with the route to the Black Sea still closed, delayed action on this decision. It was not until Stalin in January and February of 1944 grew exasperated over the failure to act on what had been agreed in principle that the problem was met by transferring some British and American ships to Soviet use as equivalent to an Italian division.

The lack of a significant voice in Italian occupation policy was another Soviet complaint Hull encountered in Moscow. Molotov presented Eden and Hull with a list of measures that the Soviet Union wanted accomplished in Italy to rid it of Fascist influences. Eden argued that many of the measures advocated by the Russians were already being put into effect by the Anglo-American occupation. The conferees agreed to issue a declaration that set forth the principles of Allied policy on Italy. Its interpretation and application remained, however, in the hands of the Commander in Chief General Eisenhower, as instructed by the Anglo-American Combined Chiefs of Staff, preventing the Soviet Union from playing too active a role for Western interests.

DECLARATION REGARDING ITALY, OCTOBER 30, 1943

The Foreign Secretaries of the United States of America, the United Kingdom and the Soviet Union have established that their three Governments are in complete agreement that Allied policy towards Italy must be based upon the fundamental principle that Fascism and all its evil influences and emanations shall be utterly destroyed and that the Italian people shall be given every opportunity to establish governmental and other institutions based upon democratic principles.

The Foreign Secretaries of the United States of America and the United Kingdom declare that the action of their Governments from the inception of the invasion of Italian territory, in so far as paramount military requirements have permitted, has been based upon this policy.

In the furtherance of this policy in the future the Foreign Secretaries of the three Governments are agreed that the following measures are important and should be put into effect:

1. It is essential that the Italian Government should be made more democratic by the introduction of representatives of those sections of the Italian people who have always opposed Fascism.

2. Freedom of speech, of religious worship, of political belief, of the press and of public meeting shall be restored in full measure to the Italian people, who shall also be entitled to form anti-Fascist political groups.

3. All institutions and organizations created by the Fascist regime shall be suppressed.

4. All Fascist or pro-Fascist elements shall be removed from the administration and from the institutions and organizations of a public character.

5. All political prisoners of the Fascist regime shall be released and accorded a full amnesty.

6. Democratic organs of local government shall be created.

7. Fascist chiefs and other persons known or suspected to be war criminals shall be arrested and handed over to justice.

In making this declaration the three Foreign Secretaries recognize that so long as active military operations continue in Italy the time at which it is possible to give full effect to the principles set out above will be determined by the Commander-in-Chief on the basis of instructions received through the Combined Chiefs of Staff. The three Governments parties to this declaration will at the request of any one of them consult on this matter.

It is further understood that nothing in this resolution is to operate against the right of the Italian people ultimately to choose their own form of government.

The primary American objective at Moscow, the signing of the Four Power declaration, met with repeated Russian objections on the grounds that the Chinese were absent and could not, therefore, be signatories. Hull, while acclaiming China as a great power, also made it obvious that the Chiang government was prepared to sign any statement the Big Three drafted for the sake of being accorded a measure of equality. Molotov finally accepted this argument, the draft was completed, and the Chinese Ambassador to Moscow signed for his government.

While the Russians and the British found the general intent of the Declaration to be acceptable, both suggested a number of changes in the American draft. Eden found inconsistency in a statement that recognized the "sovereign equality of all nations" and then proclaimed the intention of the Four Policemen to act in behalf of the community of nations. A modifying clause was introduced into the final wording, which stated that the Big Four would consult with each other but "as occasion requires" with other members of the United Nations as well. The only important change Molotov suggested dealt with point six, which provided for the use of military forces within other states only after "joint consultation and agreement." The latter words would have provided each with a veto on the other's use of armed forces outside of the national territory, and both Hull and Eden agreed to remove "and agreement."

Hull was cheered by the Soviet acceptance of his statement of principles and was confident that it meant a major gain for the American program for the postwar world. He was similarly pleased by Soviet approval of an American statement on the future treatment of Germany. It provided for the dissolution of the Nazi Party, disarmament, and reparations. Partition was not mentioned, but "decentralization of the German political structure" was to be considered along with any movement that diminished Prussia's role in the Reich. Frontier questions were to be dealt with later.

The German statement was not one of policy but referred to the creation of the conference, the European Advisory Commission. To be composed of the representatives of the three powers

THE MOSCOW DECLARATION ON GENERAL SECURITY

. . . THE GOVERNMENTS of the United States of America, the United Kingdom, the Soviet Union and China: united in their determination, in accordance with the Declaration by the United Nations of January 1, 1942, and subsequent declarations, to continue hostilities against those Axis powers with which they respectively are at war until such powers have laid down their arms on the basis of unconditional surrender; conscious of their responsibility to secure the liberation of themselves and the peoples allied with them from the menace of aggression; recognizing the necessity of ensuring a rapid and orderly transition from war to peace and of establishing and maintaining international peace and security with the least diversion of the world's human and economic resources for armaments; jointly declare:

1. That their united action, pledged for the prosecution of the war against their respective enemies, will be continued for the organization and maintenance of peace and security.

2. That those of them at war with a common enemy will act together in all matters relating to the surrender and disarmament of that enemy.

3. That they will take all measures deemed by them to be necessary to provide against any violation of the terms imposed upon the enemy.

4. That they recognize the necessity of establishing at the earliest practicable date a general international organization, based on the principle of the sovereign equality of all peace-loving states, and open to membership by all such states, large and small, for the maintenance of international peace and security.

5. That for the purpose of maintaining international peace and security pending the reestablishment of law and order and the inauguration of a system of general security, they will consult with one another and as occasion requires with other members of the United Nations with a view to joint action on behalf of the community of nations.

6. That after the termination of hostilities they will not employ their military forces within the territories of other states except for the purposes envisaged in this declaration and after joint consultation.

7. That they will confer and co-operate with one another and with other members of the United Nations to bring about a practicable general agreement with respect to the regulation of armaments in the post-war period.

November 1, 1943.

and meet in London, the Commission was to deal with political questions in connection with the ending of the war.

The British agenda for the Moscow meeting proposed the establishment of common policy towards Persia and the resistance movements in Yugoslavia. Little progress was made in these two areas or with the British proposal to discuss the resumption of Soviet relations with the Polish government in exile. The Russians were unwilling to take that action and the subject was dropped. Eden was also unsuccessful in proposing a discussion of the differences between the general and regional responsibilities of the Big Three. The idea that any one area of Europe had a special relationship to one of his allies smelled like "spheres of influence" to Hull, and he would have none of it. This very pertinent but difficult question was thus dropped and left to Churchill and Stalin to take up away from the American presence.

All three foreign ministers felt as the conference closed that they had made some substantial achievements despite areas of nonagreement. On the closing night Stalin gave a dinner at which he seated Secretary Hull on his right and confided that the Russians would "get in and help to defeat the enemy in the Far East after German defeat." Hull noted in his memoirs that he felt strongly that "great things had been accomplished" as he boarded the plane for home. Two decades later Eden wrote in his memoirs that the meeting marked the "high tide, if not of good, at least of tolerable relations between us." Molotov published no memoirs, but a Soviet history written in the post-Stalin era had high praise for the conference:

> . . . a prominent milestone in the history of the anti-fascist coalition. It showed that international co-operation was both practicable and beneficial. Its decisions facilitated the struggle of progressives for the democratic arrangement of the postwar world.

It was a favorable prelude to the meeting of the Big Three at Teheran.

In his quest for a meeting with Stalin, Roosevelt had expressed his preference for a conference without Churchill. The

British Prime Minister had already talked with Stalin in Moscow, and Roosevelt developed a number of arguments why a Russo-American leaders conference was of first priority. Churchill was strongly opposed to being excluded and cabled Roosevelt late in June of 1943 that "the whole world is expecting" a Big Three meeting. Enemy propaganda would make much of Britain's absence, which would be "serious and vexatious," while many people would be "alarmed and bewildered" to have Britain left on the sidelines. Roosevelt persisted in his plans, nevertheless, until it was Stalin who suggested a three-power meeting.

Even this conference seemed unlikely, due to Stalin's reluctance to travel any further from Moscow than Teheran. Roosevelt decided that he would still promote a conference, particularly since his doctor urged a sea voyage. In late October he suggested meeting Churchill again in North Africa and inviting Chiang Kai-shek. The place was finally set for Cairo. When Stalin agreed to Teheran, Churchill pressed for some Anglo-American discussions at Cairo before meeting the Soviet leader. Roosevelt was determined to avoid any appearance of arranging a joint front against the Russians and invited Soviet delegates to Cairo over the strong opposition of Churchill. He also planned to make the discussions with Chiang the center of the meeting in Egypt.

The President traveled across the Atlantic on the battleship *Iowa* and then flew from Algeria, where he met General Eisenhower, to Egypt. His conversations with the Chinese leader and his military staff ran from November 22 to the 26th, to the discomfort of Churchill, who wanted to send Chiang Kai-shek and his wife off to see the pyramids. But Roosevelt was interested in easing the discontent of the Chinese over the limited amount of supplies and support given them for the war against Japan. The American strategy was devoted primarily to an island-hopping movement that was eventually to bring air strength within easy striking distance of Japan. This meant a low priority for the slow-moving, largely defensive Chinese war effort on the mainland. Since Japan controlled China's seaports, supplies had to be flown in to Chiang's forces at great expense in men and machines.

Roosevelt also discussed political matters with Chiang, but their content is for the most part unknown. Madame Chiang served as translator for both her husband and the President, and Roosevelt, disregarding good diplomatic practice, made no notes of the views expressed or of agreements reached. The chief product of the conference was the Cairo Declaration, which stated that Japan would be stripped of the Pacific Islands acquired during World War I and that Manchuria, Formosa, and the Pescadores would be restored to China. The Koreans were promised that "in due course" their country would become free and independent. A trusteeship under American, Chinese, and Russian control was Roosevelt's intention for Korea during an interim period, which he said might last for forty years. Whether Chiang objected to Soviet participation in this part of Asia was unrecorded. Roosevelt also discussed the question of trusteeships in Asia and later said that Churchill had agreed to restore Hong Kong to China with the condition that the Chinese pledge within three days to announce that it would be a free port. No one in Hong Kong was to lose his property, a further condition. Churchill in his memoirs takes no note of any such agreement, for which there appears to be no record. The British Prime Minister was unhappy that the Anglo-American talks were "sadly distracted by the Chinese story," which he considered "lengthy, complicated and minor." The war against Japan the British considered to be a sideshow until the European war was won.

Roosevelt arrived at the capital of Iran on November 27 from Cairo, bringing with him his Joint Chiefs of Staff, Harry Hopkins, and the ambassadors to Britain and the U.S.S.R., Winant and Harriman. The American embassy was located at some distance from the British and the Russian, security arrangements were inadequate, assassination plots were rumored, and risk was incurred in the President's travel though the city to the other two embassies. Roosevelt therefore accepted Stalin's invitation to move to the large Russian embassy with his staff, only a block from the British. Stalin moved to one of the smaller buildings within the compound. What a century or so earlier might have been an almost insuperable protocol question was never raised. For convenience, all plenary meetings were held in a large room at the Russian embassy, and Roosevelt's cooks moved in with their kitchens to prepare the first formal dinner which the President gave for the heads of state. For both Roosevelt and Churchill, the meeting was used also as a family gathering as Roosevelt's eldest son Elliott and son-in-law John Boettiger joined him, while Churchill's daughter Sara and son Randolph were in the British party.

Four plenary sessions were held from November 28 through December 1 in addition to dinner sessions and private meetings by Roosevelt with Stalin and Churchill with Stalin. Informality was dominant, no questions of precedence were raised, and in the formal pictures Roosevelt was seated between Churchill and Stalin. Although the Russians were considered to be the hosts, the President opened the first meeting of what he called "a family circle" by virtue of his claim to be the youngest of the three leaders. Even an agenda was dispensed with to the distress of some of the staff and with some resulting rambling from topic to topic by the three leaders.

Most of the sessions were devoted to military matters rather than to political questions and principally to OVERLORD. Churchill spent some time in discussing other Mediterranean operations as preliminaries to the cross-Channel invasion, but in the end he accepted the position held by Stalin and Roosevelt that nothing should be undertaken that could lead to the further postponement of the move into France. At the close of the meetings, all three signed a statement that "took note" that OVERLORD would be launched during May of 1944 in conjunction with an operation against southern France. Stalin said that Soviet forces would launch an offensive at about the same time to prevent German forces from being moved to the Western Front. They also agreed that it was desirable that Turkey should come into the war by the end of 1943.

No firm settlements were reached on the many political questions discussed although the outlines of eventual agreements became in many cases clear. Of these, the Polish issue ranks among the most important. In both Washington and London the Polish government in exile had pressed for a championing of their case against the Russians. In the United States the celebration of the twenty-fifth anniversary of the founding of the Polish republic was used in late November to appeal to the Roosevelt administration for action. "All Americans insist on a Square Deal for Poland" was the slogan selected, and Poland was praised for its alleged historic role as a bulwark of European civilization against the Asian hordes and for saving France from surprise attack by its sacrifice of September 1939.

Churchill was the first to mention Poland to Stalin at the dinner given by Roosevelt on their first evening in Teheran. While Britain was committed to the re-establishment of a strong and independent Poland, Churchill took note of Stalin's interest in moving the Polish borders westward to the Oder River. Churchill indicated that he would like to see Poland moved westward as a unit, thus extending the Russian frontier westward as well.

The President was not feeling well that evening and had retired when this conversation took place, but he talked about Poland to Stalin at a private meeting on the afternoon of the next day. He explained to the Russian leader that if the war was on in 1944 he might have to run again for the presidency. There were six to seven million Americans of Polish ancestry whose votes he did not want to lose. Therefore, he could not take part in any decision now on the Polish frontiers or even next winter. But the President did express an opinion about the frontiers, although exactly what he said became the subject of some disagreement.

According to the notes of Charles Bohlen, who acted as Roosevelt's translator, the President told Stalin that he "would like to see the Eastern border moved further west and the Western border moved even to the River Oder." Stalin told Churchill almost a year later that the President had agreed to the Curzon line, while expressing the hope that Lvov, east of that line, could be retained by the Poles. Ambassador Harriman, who was present at the original conversation, denied that Roosevelt had agreed to the Curzon line. Prime Minister Mikolajczyk of the Polish government in exile claimed that Roosevelt told him that he made it clear at Teheran that the Polish-Russian conflict could not be settled on the basis of the Curzon line. Roosevelt himself, however, at the Yalta Conference in February of 1945, recalled, according to Bohlen's notes, that he had said at Teheran that "he believed the American people were in general favorably inclined to the Curzon line, but he felt that a concession in regard to Lvov would have a 'salutary effect.' " Another official American version of Roosevelt's Yalta recollections was even more explicit: "As I said in Teheran, in general I am in favor of the Curzon Line."

Stalin had, it seems evident, good reason for assuming tacit American consent to a major adjustment of Poland's frontiers when Churchill took up the subject again on the last evening at Teheran. Stalin said that his government considered the 1939 frontier negotiated with the Germans "just and right," or, according to the Soviet translation, "correct." He did not want to retain any regions primarily occupied by Poles. When a map was brought out, Stalin indicated some regions within the 1939 frontier that would go back to Poland. He also said that Russia needed ice-free ports on the Baltic and wanted to include Konigsberg in East Prussia and Memel with the Soviet borders. Churchill offered a formula, omitted from the American notes, but found in the British and Russian records:

> It is thought in principle that the home of the Polish State and nation should be between the so-called Curzon Line and the line of the Oder, including for Poland East Prussia and Opeln, but the actual tracing of the frontier line requires careful study and possibly disentanglement of population at some points.

Roosevelt had asked whether a voluntary transfer of peoples from mixed areas was possible and Stalin agreed that it was. (See map, page 203.)

Churchill said that "Nothing would satisfy the Poles," but he would present these frontiers to the London government. Roosevelt expressed hope that relations would be re-established between Moscow and the London Poles. The Russians would not consider such a step, and Stalin charged the government in exile with being pro-German. As was soon apparent, the Kremlin had decided to collect a rival group of Poles with whom they would deal when the German forces were driven off Polish soil.

Roosevelt had said that he would make a moral appeal to Stalin in respect to the Baltic states, but in his private conversation with the Soviet premier the record mentions only an appeal for understanding the political problems he had with Baltic-American voters. The President accepted the *de facto* incorporation of the three states, but urged on Stalin some sort of referendum to be held after the war. He assured Stalin that he was confident that these people would want to join the Soviet Union voluntarily. Stalin only said that he understood the President's political problem and that there would be ample opportunity for the Baltic peoples to express themselves.

On Germany the three leaders still seemed in accord that some form of dismemberment of the Reich had to take place. Churchill was chiefly concerned with the separation of Prussia; Roosevelt offered a rough plan for five self-governing German regions with two strategic areas, the Kiel Canal and the Ruhr-Saar region, placed under international control. There was enough recognition of the complexity of the process of creating two or more potentially new states that it was agreed to refer the matter to the European Advisory Commission.

All agreed that Germany would be disarmed, but Stalin did not believe that this was enough for future security. He spoke of his enemies as a people who had great talents and who could easily revive within fifteen or twenty years. Germany industry could then be quickly converted to arms production, so he favored Allied control of strategic areas on or within German borders from which any recrudescence of German militarism could be blocked. To this Roosevelt agreed.

The nature of Stalin's sense of humor became the source of some disagreement in another exchange on Germany. The Russian leader spoke—some thought lightly—of the need to liquidate at least 50,000, perhaps 100,000 of the German General Staff to end

German militarism. Churchill took the statement seriously and
responded with some anger that he would rather be shot himself
than agree to such infamy. Roosevelt and Eden both thought that
Stalin was joking, and in this framework the President offered a
compromise in which only 49,000 Germans would be shot. But, as
Churchill recalls in his memoirs, Roosevelt's son Elliott also took
the proposal seriously and made a speech in which he said he was
sure that the United States Army would support Stalin's proposal.

On the subject of France, Roosevelt showed some strong
feelings, conditioned in part by his animosity toward de Gaulle.
En route to Teheran, the President told his aides that the British
really wanted to build up France into a first-class power to be used
as an ally, but he did not believe that France would regain its
power status for at least twenty-five years. When he spoke privately to Stalin, he said that no Frenchman over forty and no one
who had ever taken part in the present French government should
be allowed to return to an official position in the future. Stalin
agreed that the French ruling classes were not entitled to any
benefits in the peace and that France should be punished for its
collaboration with Germany. When these views were presented to
Churchill, he defended France and said he could not think of a
civilized world without a flourishing and lively France. Stalin
replied that France could be a charming and pleasant country, but
should not be allowed to return to an important power role. Stalin
and Roosevelt agreed that France should be stripped of its colonies
and strategic holdings. Eden, after stressing Britain's concern for
the restoration of France, suggested that the French might voluntarily place their bases under some form of United Nations control
as a contribution to the peace, which would still not hurt their
pride.

Roosevelt referred to French Indo-China in discussing his
trusteeship concept with Stalin and charged that its inhabitants
were worse off after a hundred years of French rule than they had
been before. But, under a trusteeship, he believed they could be
prepared for independence within twenty to thirty years. The
British possessions, the President felt, would be a more difficult

issue, and he warned Stalin against raising the question of India with Churchill. Privately the President told the Russian leader that he thought the best solution for India would be "reform from the bottom, somewhat on the Soviet line." Stalin, more realistically, said that reform from the bottom would mean revolution.

When the discussion touched on colonies in Churchill's presence, the latter said that Britain did not want any new territory, but intended to hold on to what it had; nothing could be taken away without a war. A portion of the British Empire might eventually be released, but this would be done by Britain according to her own moral precepts. Roosevelt, according to the available records, remained silent, but Stalin said that he favored an increase in British holdings, particularly from Spanish territory around Gibraltar since the Spanish dictator Franco had been no friend of Britain or the United States.

Within the trusteeship framework Roosevelt offered two contributions to Russian interests. In the Far East he mentioned Dairen, close to Port Arthur in Manchuria, as a future free port under international guarantee, serving as an ice-free exit on the Pacific for the Russians. The exit to the Black Sea, the Straits, Roosevelt said should be open to the commerce and fleets of the world. Under the Montreux Convention of 1936 the Turks were able to close the Straits to warships when they considered themselves threatened by war and were also authorized to restrict merchant shipping under certain conditions. The control of access to the Black Sea in wartime had long been a Tsarist ambition. If this old interest slumbered, it was awakened by Churchill's suggestion that Turkey's failure to join the Allies might have serious political and territorial consequences. When Molotov inquired of Eden what Churchill meant and received no satisfactory answer, Stalin raised the matter. Churchill then said that it would be an awkward time to raise such issues while the Allies were still trying to induce the Turks to join the war but with Roosevelt's agreement it was to be considered later.

The nature of a new international organization was still a matter of minor interest at Teheran, but Roosevelt did expand to some extent his own thinking on the subject. In a private conversation with Stalin, he now suggested, along with the Four Policemen, an executive committee composed of one British Dominion, one Asian nation, one Middle Eastern, one Latin-American and two European states, along with the Big Four. This body would be authorized only to make recommendations, while the power to deal with threats to the peace would remain in the hands of the Policemen.

Stalin objected in behalf of the small nations of Europe, which he said would not like the role assigned to the Four Policemen and would in particular resent Chinese power applied in Europe. Stalin did not think that China would attain major power status at the end of the war. As a possible alternative, Stalin suggested three regional committees, one each for Europe, the Far East and the Americas. Churchill had also made this suggestion to Roosevelt and added that he wanted the United States also to be a member of the European committee. Roosevelt was doubtful about this possibility. American isolationism was too strong, he told Stalin, to permit the United States to be a member of an organization dealing with purely European matters and yet able to call on American troops for action. The President was then asked whether the Four Policemen could count on American manpower, and Roosevelt was dubious. He said he envisioned the British and Russians providing the armies, while the United States would contribute air and naval power. American air forces could then take part in the bombing of peace-breaking nations when necessary, but the President thought that in some instances it would be enough to quarantine a nation that was a threat to the peace. American unwillingness to take part in a purely European organization seems to have impressed Stalin. He later told the President that after thinking it over he favored a worldwide rather than a regional organization to keep the peace.

Roosevelt returned to Cairo very much pleased with his first personal encounter with Stalin. Before the Conference closed, the Soviet Premier had assured him that his country would join the war against Japan after the defeat of Germany. The joint communiqué for the press expressed the President's feelings in its closing sentences, "We came here with hope and determination. We leave here, friends in fact, in spirit and purpose."

When Hull returned from the Moscow Foreign Ministers' Conference, he addressed a joint session of Congress in terms that expressed great optimism. When the Declaration of Four Nations on General Security went into effect, he believed:

> . . . there will no longer be need for spheres of influence, for alliances, for balance of power, or any other of the special arrangements through which, in the unhappy past, the nations strove to safeguard their security or to promote their interests.

The Wilsonian vision of a world of sovereign states without conflicting national interests had come alive again. Hull failed to see that even his own favorite panacea for the world's problems, free trade by means of reciprocal trade agreements, was a program that only the minority of strong, industrialized economies favored. For other nations it was frequently seen as a means by which the rich nations dominated the economies of the poor.

At Teheran the three leaders had discussed a radical remaking of Europe, justified, as nations had claimed in the past, by their status as victors with overwhelming military power. And if Roosevelt had his way, the new international organization was going to be one in which only four nations held real power. Yet, as he told Americans on his return in a radio address on December 24:

> The rights of every nation, large or small, must be respected and guarded as jealously as are the rights of every individual within our own republic. The doctrine that the strong shall dominate the weak is the doctrine of our enemies—and we reject it.

These ideals, the President recognized, were not enough.

> But, at the same time, we are agreed that if force is necessary to keep international peace, international force will be applied— for as long as it may be necessary.

This force was to be exerted in behalf of the rights of all nations by four powers, no one of which had as yet experienced that miracle of transformation by which the interests and aspirations of the peoples they claimed to represent took priority over their own interests as sovereign states. This dilemma was inevitable, given the structure of the international state system and the war-weary desire for future co-operation on peaceful terms. Danger lay in the failure of the leaders to recognize the incompatibilities in the dual roles that they were claiming for their nations. This may have led a *Life* magazine editorial writer to comment sourly on the glowing words of the Teheran communiqué, which spoke of winning "an enduring Peace" and the elimination of "tyranny and slavery, oppression and intolerance." Said *Life:* "If it can be believed, it solves everything; if it cannot, it is a colossal fraud."

Poland, Germany, and Yalta: 1944–45

Fourteen months passed between the first meeting of the Big Three in November of 1943 and their second meeting in the Crimea in February of 1945. In that interval the military situation had changed drastically in favor of the Allies. The defeat of Germany appeared to be a certainty within a year. The Anglo-American forces had invaded France on June 6, 1944, and taken Paris by August 25. The Battle of the Bulge in December of 1944 had set back the push into Germany, but General Marshall reported to the Big Three that the Rhine would be crossed in early March of 1945. On the Soviet Front the advance was even greater. Finland signed an armistice with the Russians in September of 1944, and Rumania did likewise the same month. Bulgaria agreed to an armistice in October and Hungary in January of 1945. The former Baltic states, East Prussia, and most of Poland were in Russian control by early February, and the Red Army had crossed the Oder in its drive toward Berlin. In the Pacific, the American advance had reached the Philippines, while the Japanese home islands were taking heavier and heavier bombings from the American Super-Fortresses.

During the fourteen months between the meetings, Roosevelt and Churchill had kept in direct touch with Stalin as well as communicating through their ambassadors. According to the published Soviet records, Churchill had sent over one hundred messages to the Soviet Premier and Roosevelt over fifty. Almost half of this correspondence dealt with military matters, but some attempts were made to cope with political issues. Churchill and Roosevelt also met once in the interval, their second Quebec Conference, September 11 to 16, 1944, while Churchill made his second trip to talk with Stalin at the Kremlin in October of 1944.

Poland remained the dominant political issue in the discussions between Washington and Moscow from Teheran to Yalta. The Polish government in exile grew desperate as the Russian forces began to occupy Polish soil and their authority remained unrecognized by Moscow. Marshal Pilsudski, who had ruled Poland with a strong hand until 1935, based his foreign policy on the motto, "romanticism in aims and realism in method." The London Poles continued to work on the same premises, only frequently forsaking realism in their methods. Just before the opening of the Teheran Conference, both Roosevelt and Churchill received a lengthy memorandum from the government in exile that contained a threat of war against the Soviet Union if the Red Army crossed on to Polish territory before recognizing the authority of the London government. Churchill took upon himself the task, after Teheran, to convince his Polish guests that they would have to accept a major readjustment of their eastern frontiers in order to secure renewed Soviet recognition. Roosevelt gave some limited support to the Prime Minister, who was able, with Stalin's encouragement, to promise the Poles territorial compensations in the West.

On February 22, 1944, Churchill told Parliament that he found the Russian proposals for the Polish frontier "reasonable" and "just." The Polish exiles, headed by Prime Minister Stanislaw Mikolajczyk, rejected completely any territorial changes in favor of Moscow. Mikolajczyk then approached President Roosevelt in the hope that the United States would take up the defense of the Polish cause against the Kremlin. The President, preparing for his unprecedented fourth term campaign, was unwilling to take a

public stand that would offend the Polish-American voter, but he
was also unwilling to offend the Soviet Union at a time when he
sought their co-operation in the postwar organization. He managed
to delay the visit until June of 1944, when the Polish leader
arrived in Washington.

The only available record of their conversation is that published by the Poles. Roosevelt reportedly blamed the suggestion for
the Curzon line on Churchill and claimed that he was opposed to
its use in drafting the new boundary. He said, according to the
Poles, that he was not worried about the territorial settlement and
that Poland would get East Prussia and Silesia if they gave up "a
little something somewhere else." Mikolajczyk told Eden later that
Roosevelt promised to help the Poles at an appropriate time to
retain Lvov, the oil areas of eastern Galicia, and even to acquire
Königsberg, which Stalin had clearly marked for Russian annexation at Teheran. Eden commented to the Foreign Office that "the
poor Poles are sadly deluding themselves if they place any faith in
these vague and generous promises."

With his faith in the importance of personal diplomacy,
Roosevelt believed that a man-to-man contact between Mikolajczyk
and Stalin would be helpful in dealing with the Polish problem.
An appeal was sent to Moscow for such a meeting in which the
President assured Stalin that he was not pressing upon him "my
personal views in a matter which is of special concern to you and
your country." Stalin agreed to the meeting, and Roosevelt could
claim the gratitude of the Poles for making the arrangements
without taking a position in direct conflict with the Russians.

By the time Mikolajczyk reached Moscow at the end of July
1944, the Russians had adopted a new policy. A carefully selected
group of Poles had been gathered in the "Polish Committee of
National Liberation," which was to carry out civil government on
Polish territory turned over to them by the Red Army after the
Germans retreated. Stalin was then able to face the London Poles
with a rival group that he claimed represented the new Poland of
younger men. Mikolajczyk was told that his government would
have to join forces with the new Committee, located in Lublin, to

form a provisional government to be recognized by the Soviet Union. The London Polish leader was unable to make any progress during his visit in getting the Russians to change their views on the boundary question and could only return to his exile post empty-handed.

Churchill saw the Polish question along with other Eastern European issues as becoming a dangerous threat to Allied unity and paid his second visit to Stalin in October of 1944. He brought with him Mikolajczyk, and Ambassador Harriman attended the meetings as an "observer" to preserve an appearance of American noninvolvement.

With the encouragement of Churchill and Stalin, Mikolajczyk met with representatives of the Lublin Poles, but he could reach no agreement for the formation of a provisional government that would not put the representatives of the Polish government in exile in a minority position. With Russian backing, the new Committee was not prepared to share power on any basis of equality with their London rivals. Mikolajczyk's Cabinet also refused to give him the flexibility by which he could compromise on the eastern border question. His second encounter with Stalin was, consequently, fruitless.

Churchill was enraged over the London Poles' refusal to accept the fact that their position was a helpless one and to make some concessions rather than to continue their militancy in the face of Soviet power. General Wladyslaw Anders, leader of the Polish exile armies, told Churchill on one occasion that, after defeating the Germans, the Russians would be so weak that they could be beaten by the Poles. Churchill now told Mikolajczyk, "If you want to conquer Russia, we shall leave you to do it." But the British Prime Minister was unwilling to carry out his threat to wash his hands completely of the London Poles. They were, in turn, unyielding, and the Moscow meeting ended with the Polish question unresolved.

While in Moscow, Churchill also had a number of talks with Stalin without the presence of Harriman as observer, a procedure that created some concern in Washington. Before Churchill arrived

at the Kremlin, Roosevelt reminded Stalin by cable that there was
"literally no question, military or political, in which the United
States is not interested." Only the three leaders, the President said,
could find solutions to the unresolved issues. He wanted the
Churchill talks to be considered as only preliminaries to a meeting
that he would be able to attend once the November presidential
election was over. Roosevelt agreed, however, in response to
Harriman's inquiry, that it would be inadvisable for the American
ambassador to try to push his way into the Stalin-Churchill *tête-à-
têtes.*

The British Prime Minister did take up with Stalin the
question of conflicts of interest in the Balkans, where the Red
Army was victorious and where local Communist movements were
becoming political factors. Without the Americans to object,
Churchill decided to offer a practical basis for a division of influence in an area where British and Russian policies had frequently
clashed in the century before World War I. Scratching his figures
on a piece of paper, Churchill suggested a 90 percent Russian
interest in Rumania, balanced by a 90 percent British interest in
Greece. Bulgaria was to be in the Soviet sphere, but with a 75
percent to 25 percent division with Britain. Yugoslavia and Hungary were to be nations in which influence was shared 50–50.
Stalin readily accepted this kind of bargain and made a large tick
on the paper to indicate his agreement. The Soviet forces were
already in occupation of Bulgaria and parts of Hungary so that
there was no danger that the British interest would prove a serious
obstacle to Soviet interest. Churchill in his memoirs states that this
division dealt only with "immediate wartime arrangements," but
he knew that it would most likely affect the peacetime Balkans as
well.

In May of 1944 Ambassador Halifax approached Secretary
Hull to get his reaction to a proposed Anglo-Russian agreement,
recognizing each other's predominant role in Greece and Rumania.
Hull was assured that this was not a division of spheres of influence nor would the arrangement affect the rights of the powers at
the peace conference. But the Secretary was flatly opposed to any

such bargain. Churchill then appealed directly to Roosevelt, who said that such an arrangement would be acceptable for a three-month trial period. The State Department had objected when Roosevelt consulted them; the President then acted without informing the Department, while Hull continued to send his protests to London. Churchill, however, found his bargain with Moscow in one respect a very useful one. As the British forces occupied Greece, they crushed with force the Greek Communist movement and its allies without protest from Moscow.

While Poland and the Balkans were the important political subjects of the October 1944 Moscow Conference, Germany had occupied a large part of the attention of Churchill and Roosevelt at Quebec the previous September. As the conquest of France neared completion, the policies to be followed in occupying Germany became urgent. The European Advisory Commission, composed of the American and Soviet ambassadors to London and Sir William Strang of the British Foreign Office, had limited authority. When it began its meetings in January of 1944, it soon decided to refer major matters back to the three heads of government for decision.

What became an important political matter, the division of Germany into occupation zones, was settled largely in terms of military considerations. Roosevelt originally was strongly of the opinion that the United States should avoid as much as possible the problem of supplying its forces through France and the use of French ports. This could be done by so dividing Germany that the Americans would handle the northwestern sector and use Bremen and Hamburg as its ports for receiving supplies. The British would occupy the southern sector and handle the problem of de Gaulle and the new French government. The allocation of armies in the OVERLORD operation, however, placed the Americans to the south, and as these armies neared the Rhine the problem of switching appeared so complex that Roosevelt settled for the southern sector of Germany. The Russians were naturally to have the eastern zone, and the dividing line, according to both British and Russian proposals in early 1944, was to run about two hundred miles to the west of Berlin. The Americans raised no objections to this proposed division with the capital of the Reich, Berlin, expected to be under joint administration of the three victors. Until late in the war the War Department considered that all of Germany up to the Rhine might be in the hands of the Red Army at the end of the fighting and that the United States and Britain would acquire a zone only on Soviet sufferance. The Soviet proposal of February 1944, which accepted a zone of little more than a third of Germany, was viewed as an act of generous co-operation when the only American troops on the European continent were stalled on the Italian peninsula.

Beyond agreement on zones of occupation, there were in the fall of 1944 still no arrangements completed between London and Washington as to how the Germans were to be treated under occupation. The President was initially largely responsible for this procrastination. On October 20, 1944, he wrote to Hull, "I dislike making detailed plans for a country which we do not yet occupy." In Britain the Chiefs of Staff worked on the assumption that Germany would be dismembered, not only to prevent German rearmament as a nation, but also to guard against any future powerful Russo-German alliance. The military planners in 1944 were already considering the organization of northwestern and southern Germany into a strong unit against a Soviet Union strengthened by the support of eastern Germany. The British Foreign Office was not only opposed to such preparations for a divided Europe, but was also skeptical of the policy of dismemberment. German nationalism was expected in time to protest forced disunity and to win strong support from public opinion in the West.

In Washington some important political matters were in the process of being decided by the War Department without regard to the role of the State Department. SHAEF, Supreme Headquarters, Allied Expeditionary Force, completed a handbook for military government in June of 1944 in which the chief consideration was to ease the task of the occupation forces. The German political and economic system was to be disturbed as little as possible; some light and heavy industry was to be rehabilitated, and the German standard of living was to be maintained at a considerably higher level than in surrounding countries. This sort of treatment was claimed to be in accord with the directives of the Combined Chiefs of Staff, although General Eisenhower was to some degree at odds with this program in the summer of 1944. He favored a harsher policy and saw the advocates of a "soft peace" as really advocating the creation of a strong western Germany as a bulwark against the Soviet Union.

Secretary of Treasury Henry Morgenthau Jr. became the spearhead of the "hard peace" movement with the support of many Americans whose relatives had died in Hitler's mass extermination program. When Morgenthau discovered in August of 1944 that the State Department had prepared a statement opposing the partitioning of Germany and supporting only mild action against the German economy, he began the drafting of an alternative program in his department. He also acquired a copy of the Army military government handbook and took it to Roosevelt to protest its policies.

The President inclined strongly towards the "hard peace" position and ordered the War Department to withdraw its occupation handbook. As he told Morgenthau, he didn't want the Germans to starve, but he thought it would be sufficient to feed them three times a day from Army soup kitchens. On this program they could be kept healthy, yet impressed with the fact that they were part of a defeated nation. It was not only the Nazi leaders who must be punished. "The German people as a whole must have it driven home to them that the whole nation has been engaged in a lawless conspiracy against the decencies of modern civilization," Roosevelt wrote Secretary of War Stimson in late August of 1944.

Encouraged by the President's toughness, Morgenthau led his aides in writing a program that would eliminate Germany as a factor in the world economy. German industry was to be dismantled and sent abroad as reparations, German mines were to be closed permanently, and all German assets abroad confiscated. Britain and Russia, Morgenthau thought, would thrive on Germany's former customers. German labor would also be used as reparations, and the millions left unemployed by the destruction of industry could be sent to work on reclamation and hydroelectric projects all over the world. The Morgenthau plan was completed in early September and ran into immediate opposition from Secretaries Stimson and Hull. It was "just fighting brutality with brutality," Stimson said, turning Germany into a ghost territory and poisoning the future of the peace.

The debate was carried to the White House, where on September 6, 1944 all three Secretaries argued their case before the President with Hull and Stimson generally on the same side. Roosevelt had no basic objections to turning the economic clock back to 1810 for Germany and spoke romantically of how comfortable life had been in the area of his Hyde Park home at that date. But he also gave some heed to Stimson's argument that the Morgenthau plan was, in the analogy of Charles Lamb, burning the house down in order to get roast pig. The meeting ended inconclusively, although some immediate changes were made in the Army occupation handbook. It limited the degree of economic rehabilitation to that immediately necessary to the occupation forces, ordered relief supplies to be kept at the minimum necessary to prevent disease and disorder, and stated that Nazi officials must be removed regardless of occupation expediencies.

It promised something of a victory for Morgenthau when he was suddenly invited by the President to attend the conference with Churchill at Quebec. The invitation seemed even more surprising when the Secretary of the Treasury learned that neither Hull nor Hopkins would be present. At dinner on his first evening in Quebec, the Secretary was given his opportunity to explain his plan for Germany. Churchill's initial reaction was one of rage; he said that he looked upon the plan as he would look upon the prospect of chaining himself to a dead German. Morgenthau was rebuffed by the intensity of the Prime Minister's hostile reaction.

The next day Churchill had changed his mind. He agreed to having Lord Cherwell, his scientific adviser, join Morgenthau in drafting a statement for conference approval. The result was not to the Prime Minister's liking, but he used the draft as a basis for a memorandum that he dictated on the treatment of Germany. Without any debate and to Morgenthau's great satisfaction, Churchill and the President then signed it.

⎰THE QUEBEC AGREEMENT ON GERMANY⎱

At a conference between the President and the Prime Minister upon the best measures to prevent renewed rearmament by Germany, it was felt that an essential feature was the future disposition of the Ruhr and the Saar. The ease with which the metallurgical, chemical and electrical industries in Germany can be converted from peace to war has already been impressed upon us by bitter experience. It must also be remembered that the Germans have devastated a large portion of the industries of Russia, and of other neighboring Allies, and it is only in accordance with justice that these injured countries should be entitled to remove the machinery they require in order to repair the losses they have suffered. The industries referred to in the Ruhr and in the Saar would therefore be necessarily put out of action and closed down. It was felt that the two districts should be put under some body under the world organization which would supervise the dismantling of these industries and make sure that they were not started up again by some subterfuge.

This program for eliminating the war-making industries in the Ruhr and in the Saar is looking forward to converting Germany into a country primarily agricultural and pastoral in its character.

The Prime Minister and the President were in agreement upon this programme.

OK

F.D.R.
W.S.C.

September 15, 1944

There was some consternation in both Washington and London when Morgenthau's success with his "hard peace" plan became known. To Secretary of War Stimson, it appeared "as an open confession of the bankruptcy of hope for a reasonable economic and political settlement of the causes of war." To Hull, as he stated in his memoirs, it was a plan of "blind vengeance" that would "arouse the eternal resentment of the Germans" and in its economic effects punish all of Europe. Eden, who attended the Quebec Conference, protested Churchill's signing of a document that so completely contradicted other decisions, but only succeeded in arousing Churchill's ire. As the Foreign Minister later noted in his memoirs, it was the only occasion he remembers on which the Prime Minister showed impatience with his cabinet aide's views in the presence of foreigners.

When Morgenthau returned to Washington he believed that it was the prospect of taking over Germany's customers that won Churchill's consent to the destruction of German industry. In London the Foreign Office was quick to point to the economic realities. As John Maynard Keynes had stated in 1919 in his *Economic Consequences of the Peace,* a Germany incapable of exporting manufactures would also be incapable of buying imports, thus eliminating a very valuable British market. Some American observers at Quebec suspected Churchill of being anxious to have the Secretary of the Treasury's support in the current Lend-Lease negotiations. Arrangements were being made for Phase II of Lend-Lease, for the period after the defeat of Germany and before the defeat of Japan when Britain would still need American financial support on a generous level.

As a member of Parliament in 1949 Churchill discussed his action at Quebec and claimed that the document had been signed *ad referendum* and became null when it failed to get approval of the Foreign Office and the Department of State. He was, however, sorry that he had signed it. In his final volume of memoirs, written four years later, he passed quickly over the subject of the Morgenthau plan, leaving the reader with the impression that he had considered but not approved of the idea of "pastoralizing" Germany, the word that he himself had contributed to the final draft.

Roosevelt, like Churchill, was quick to push aside the significance of his action in signing the September 15 statement. He gave Hull the impression on his return that he had not committed himself to Morgenthau's proposals. A few days later he told

Stimson that he had no idea of how he could have initialed a statement that went far beyond his intentions in respect to the German economy. At the same time the President thought of himself as an opponent of the "soft peace" advocates. As he wrote to Senator Kenneth McKellar of Tennessee in late August of 1944:

> It is amazing how many people are beginning to get soft in the future terms of the Germans and Japs. I fear it is going to be a real trouble for us next year or the year after.

At Yalta the following February, one of Roosevelt's first remarks to Stalin was that he was "more bloodthirsty" on the subject of the Germans than he had been the year previously. He said that he hoped the Russian leader would again propose the toast that had shocked Churchill at Teheran, to the execution of 50,000 German Army officers.

The second Big Three meeting and the last for Roosevelt opened on February 3, 1945. Stalin's reluctance to travel far from Moscow again determined the location in the resort town of Yalta in the Crimea. The American delegation was housed in a former winter palace of the Tsars, aided in supply and communications by some Allied naval vessels in the Black Sea, the first that the Turks had permitted to pass through the Straits since the beginning of the war. The President had intended to take a small delegation of about thirty-five, including servants, but ended with a party of over three hundred, with the British sending an almost equally large number. Cordell Hull had resigned in ill health in November of 1944 and was replaced by Edward R. Stettinius Jr., who accompanied the President, along with Harry Hopkins and the future Secretary of State James F. Byrnes.

Roosevelt considered the meeting an urgent one because of the many issues left unsettled as the end of the war appeared in sight. Churchill had also felt that the conference was urgent, but when confronted with the Russians, both he and Roosevelt postponed action on specific proposals and called for further study.

The net results of the Yalta Conference in clear agreements was consequently small. With flagging energies and a decline in health obvious to many observers, the President still spoke of making the final agreements at some future peace conference. Then, he hoped, these details would be in accord with the position of various American interest groups and receive ready approval of the United States Senate in treaty form. In the meantime, he wanted to be certain of Russian aid in the war with Japan and of Stalin's willingness to be a co-operative member of the Four Policemen. To this end he was very cordial to Stalin while pushing off into the future as many issues as possible where Russian and American interests were likely to clash.

Churchill seemed ready to postpone some matters for a different reason. As the Red Army fought its way towards the center of Germany and occupied the Balkans, the Prime Minister's old fears of the Bolshevization of Europe began to revive as he faced the realities of Soviet power. He began to concern himself with the balance of power and the creation of strength in the West. Roosevelt spoke several times of the limited time that he could expect to keep American troops in Europe after victory, and Churchill looked to European elements to support Britain in countering Russian influence and strength. A revived France was one British goal, as well as some friendly governments in Eastern Europe and the Balkans that might show their independence once the Red Army withdrew. It was a frail hope in 1945, but Churchill from his position of weakness could only hope that time would be on his side. Delaying the political settlement might make possible the classic work of restoring a power balance.

Domestic political considerations also contributed to Churchill's policy of evading some settlements. Once Germany was defeated, the wartime political coalition in Britain would come to an end; the Labour Party would be free to attack the Tory policies it had once supported. The Prime Minister owed it to his Party not to make any concessions to Soviet strength that might be used by his opponents in the next general election.

The strategy of Stalin and his advisers at Yalta is more

difficult to describe with any degree of certainty. Unless it is assumed that he had hidden utopian Communist dreams of world conquest, it seems likely from Stalin's words and actions that he was ready and anxious to settle for a limited but definite Soviet sphere of influence in Europe. Outside of that sphere, he was willing to give the Americans and British a free hand. He accepted Roosevelt's Four Policemen concept, only dubious about the membership of China. He was also opposed to any arrangement in the new international organization whereby the control of Latin American and British Dominion votes would enable Washington and London to use the new organization to harass the Soviet Union. He felt the League had been used in this way during the first Russo-Finnish War. Difficult though it was for the Americans and British to conceive, the Russians in their international dealings had something of what the former Soviet Ambassador to London, Maisky, called an "inferiority complex." As Sir A. Clark Kerr reported from Moscow in August of 1943:

> We make them feel like country cousins and they minded because they knew they were. . . . We expected them to be as grown up and metropolitan as ourselves. They were not, and we should remember that, for it was very important.

Kerr protested Maisky's charges, but admitted, ". . . in my heart, I felt that he was right." By 1945 the crude "country cousin" was fully conscious of possessing the strongest land army in the world and facing a war-weakened Britain and a United States anxious to withdraw to the Western hemisphere.

Stalin took up the first item at the conference, Germany, with the object of reaching agreement on all major aspects of that country's future under occupation. Soviet forces were crossing the Oder River, and he claimed a readiness to discuss and settle on any common policies to be carried out. The nature of German dismemberment was his initial question and one relevant to the settlement of the tripartite zones of occupation. Both Churchill and Roosevelt had previously suggested some schemes for partitioning without going into the specifics. Although Churchill told Stalin that he agreed with partition in principle, any decision on a specific plan would require elaborate research on the "historical, political, economic and sociological aspects" of Germany. The Prime Minister spoke of the isolation of Prussia and the creation of a new southern German state with its capital possibly being located at Vienna, but the British government was not prepared to go further.

Roosevelt's response to Stalin's initiative was to give his support to partition and to express his belief that division into five or seven states would be desirable. But, like the British, the Americans were not prepared to settle on any major details. All that was agreed on was the mention of "dismemberment" in any German surrender document while deferring to the foreign ministers the task of suggesting some plan by which the problem could be studied and proposals made. Eden fought to weaken the tacit agreement on some form of dismemberment. Over Molotov's objection, it was listed only as one of the steps that the Allies would take "as they deem requisite" for future peace and security along with disarmament and demilitarization. Who was to prepare the specific plans was never agreed upon.

Agreement was reached at Yalta to give France a share in the occupation program. Churchill was the chief proponent of French interests and argued that this country deserved a geographical sector of Germany and a seat on the Allied Control Council. Roosevelt had resisted this idea strongly, continuing to express his distaste for General de Gaulle and his conviction that France would remain a minor power, disarmed and subject to the will of the Four Policemen. In private conversation with Stalin on the opening day of the Yalta Conference, the President had also tried to turn Stalin against the French. Admitting that his action was "indiscreet," he reported to the Premier that the British had the idea of "artificially building France up into a strong power" with an army that would hold the line in any future war until the British armies landed.

Roosevelt's reversal of his position seems related to his view that American troops could not be kept in Europe for more than two years after the German defeat. Churchill pointed out to him the importance of French troops in any long term occupation program, and the President conceded. Stalin had no strong objections to French participation as long as the fourth zone was carved out of the area assigned to Britain and the United States. Signing a treaty of alliance and mutual assistance with de Gaulle in December of 1944, he accepted a continuing role for Paris in European politics. The communiqué on occupation and control (see page 142) announced the inclusion of France, but made no mention of dismemberment.

The Russians also raised the reparations question to find that this was another issue that the Americans and British were still reluctant to face. Having suffered by far the worst of any nation from the German forces, the Soviet Union had the strongest interest in the economic measures against Germany that would aid its own recovery. A plan was presented that provided for reparations in kind, to be withdrawn from Germany in two ways. The first was the removal of factories, machinery, rolling stock, and other capital goods, to be completed in two years and to leave the Germans only 20 percent of their capacity in heavy industry, with complete removal of industries specialized for armaments. The second form of reparations was to be in goods, drawn from current production for no more than ten years. The totals extracted were to be divided among the victors in proportion to their contribution to the war and to their war losses. The Soviet Union estimated that its share should reach $10 billion.

Churchill now objected strongly to reparations. He cited the bad effects of this program after World War I and feared that a destitute Germany would present serious difficulties for the occupying powers. Roosevelt, however, said that he was willing to support the Soviet claims and that the United States intended to take over all German property within its borders. He also held to the view that the German standard of living should not be allowed to continue higher than that of the Soviet Union.

Molotov, with Stettinius' initial agreement, suggested that the total of reparations should be set at $20 billion, valuing the goods

COMMUNIQUÉ ON THE OCCUPATION AND CONTROL OF GERMANY

We have agreed on common policies and plans for enforcing the unconditional surrender terms which we shall impose together on Nazi Germany after German armed resistance has been finally crushed. These terms will not be made known until the final defeat of Germany has been accomplished. Under the agreed plan, the forces of the Three Powers will each occupy a separate zone of Germany. Coordinated administration and control has been provided for under the plan through a central Control Commission consisting of the Supreme Commanders of the Three Powers with headquarters in Berlin. It has been agreed that France should be invited by the Three Powers, if she should so desire, to take over a zone of occupation, and to participate as a fourth member of the Control Commission. The limits of the French zone will be agreed by the four governments concerned through their representatives on the European Advisory Commission.

It is our inflexible purpose to destroy German militarism and Nazism and to ensure that Germany will never again be able to disturb the peace of the world. We are determined to disarm and disband all German armed forces; break up for all time the German General Staff that has repeatedly contrived the resurgence of German militarism; remove or destroy all German military equipment; eliminate or control all German industry that could be used for military production; bring all war criminals to just and swift punishment and exact reparation in kind for the destruction wrought by the Germans; wipe out the Nazi party, Nazi laws, organizations and institutions, remove all Nazi and militarist influences from public office and from the cultural and economic life of the German people; and take in harmony such other measures in Germany as may be necessary to the future peace and safety of the world. It is not our purpose to destroy the people of Germany, but only when Nazism and Militarism have been extirpated will there be hope for a decent life for Germans, and a place for them in the comity of nations.

in 1938 prices, and that the Soviet Union receive approximately 50 percent. Eden in the Foreign Ministers' session opposed any mention of specific figures, and on this basis the subject was returned to the three leaders for settlement in their final session. Churchill then vetoed any setting of figures and claimed that instructions from his Cabinet required him to do so.

To avoid a stalemate, Eden suggested that the question of figures be referred to the Reparations Commission that was to be established in Moscow. The Russians replied that it was not logical to refer to a lesser body an important decision that could not be agreed upon by the three leaders. Nevertheless, the matter was referred, and the protocol only noted that the Russians and the Americans had agreed to set the $20 billion figure as a basis of discussion. Neither this, nor the decision to include German labor in reparations, an aspect in which both the British and Russians were interested, was included in the communiqué. The secret protocol was, in effect, a reversal of the Quebec agreement and discarded the goals of the Morgenthau plan. If reparations were to come out of current production, as the Soviet Union suggested, the dismantling of the German economy had to stop short of pastoralization.

Another aspect of the German question that was discussed without clear conclusion was the matter of future boundaries. France was anxious to achieve its traditional expansionist goals and to extend its territory to the left bank of the Rhine. Both Stalin and Churchill had earlier expressed their belief that the Ruhr and the Saar industrial areas should be taken from Germany and put under international control. Churchill held out for further study of Germany's future borders on the west, and settlement was postponed.

Germany's eastern frontiers were a part of the larger Polish question and discussed in relation to the controversy over the Russo-Polish border. Churchill and Roosevelt had previously approved in principle some cessions to Russia from Poland's 1938 frontiers, with compensation to be given the Poles in the West at the expense

SECRET PROTOCOL ON REPARATIONS

1. Germany must pay in kind for the losses caused by her to the Allied nations in the course of the war. Reparations are to be rece'ved in the first instance by those countries which have borne the main burden of the war, have suffered the heaviest losses and have organized victory over the enemy.

2. Reparation in kind is to be exacted from Germany in three following forms:

a) Removals within 2 years from the surrender of Germany or the cessation of organised resistance from the national wealth of Germany located on the territory of Germany herself as well as outside her territory (equipment, machine-tools, ships, rolling stock, German investments abroad, shares of industrial, transport and other enterprises in Germany etc.), these removals to be carried out chiefly for purpose of destroying the war potential of Germany.

b) Annual deliveries of goods from current production for a period to be fixed.

c) Use of German labour.

3. For the working out on the above principles of a detailed plan for exaction of reparation from Germany an Allied Reparation Commission will be set up in Moscow. It will consist of three representatives—one from the Union of Soviet Socialist Republics, one from the United Kingdom and one from the United States of America.

4. With regard to the fixing of the total sum of the reparation as well as the distribution of it among the countries which suffered from the German aggression the Soviet and American delegations agreed as follows:

"The Moscow Reparation Commission should take in its initial studies as a basis for discussion the suggestion of the Soviet Government that the total sum of the reparation in accordance with the points (*a*) and (*b*) of the paragraph 2 should be 20 billion dollars and that 50% of it should go to the Union of Soviet Socialist Republics."

The British delegation was of the opinion that pending consideration of the reparation question by the Moscow Reparation Commission no figures of reparation should be mentioned.

The above Soviet-American proposal has been passed to the Moscow Reparation Commission as one of the proposals to be considered by the Commission.

of Germany. Churchill at Teheran had spoken of Poland's western boundary being the line of the Oder River which ran northwestward and then north from its source in the mountains of Silesia. Stalin now stood for the line of the Oder and the western Neisse River, which branched off the Oder and ran due south, adding a large segment of Silesia to future Poland.

Churchill's initial concern was over the millions of Germans who lived in the area to be annexed. He said that he did not want "to stuff the Polish goose until it dies of German indigestion." Stalin assured him that the Germans had already fled to escape the advancing Russian armies. Churchill then spoke of the room that would presumably be available in Germany for these refugees who would fill the places of the war dead. Roosevelt's concern was to avoid any agreement on this frontier that was specific enough to be a treaty and thus require Senate consideration. The American delegation did submit a proposal that accepted the line of the Oder, but said that there would "appear to be little justification" for the extension to the western Neisse. Churchill said that his Cabinet could not accept the Neisse. The boundary question was left at that point, and the communiqué said only that Poland would receive "substantial accessions of territory in the North and West," but that final delimitation would await the peace conference.

There was less debate over Poland's eastern frontier. Both Churchill and Roosevelt agreed that it would roughly approximate the Curzon line, but both wanted some exceptions in favor of the Poles. Roosevelt appealed to Stalin to give the Poles Lvov, because of its large Polish population, and because, as he said, it would make it easier for him "at home." Churchill seconded this effort; it would be an act of magnanimity by the Soviet Union and acclaimed as such. Stalin was unmovable. If a favorable frontier was a matter of honor for the Poles, he said, it was both honor and security to the Russians, who had twice in thirty years been attacked on this frontier. In giving Bialystok Province to the Poles, he was already doing what Lenin had opposed in 1920. "Should we be less Russian than Curzon and Clemenceau?" Stalin asked, referring to the two men who had supported in 1920 the frontier he now claimed.

Churchill and Roosevelt could do little at this point. They accepted a statement that said that Poland's eastern frontier should follow the Curzon line with some digressions in favor of Poland. At the last moment Roosevelt succeeded in weakening the statement somewhat by substituting the word "consider" for "agree" as the verb expressing the position of the three governments.

COMMUNIQUÉ ON POLISH BOUNDARY

The three Heads of Government consider that the Eastern frontier of Poland should follow the Curzon Line with digressions from it in some regions of five to eight kilometres in favour of Poland. They recognise that Poland must receive substantial accessions of territory in the North and West. They feel that the opinion of the new Polish Provisional Government of National Unity should be sought in due course on the extent of these accessions and that the final delimitation of the Western frontier of Poland should thereafter await the Peace Conference.

The most difficult and most persistently troublesome issue at Yalta was the composition of the Polish government, which was to be recognized by all three powers. Russian occupation forces were restoring a large measure of civil authority and assigning some of it to the Lublin provisional government. This action and the Soviet attitude toward the Warsaw uprising had added greatly to the bitterness of the London Poles. The uprising had taken place in August and September of 1944 as the Red Army approached the Polish capital, an attempt by the underground forces to be in possession of Warsaw when the Russians arrived. The Russians had stopped short of Warsaw, in the face of stiff German resistance, but probably for political reasons as well, while Hitler's forces ruthlessly restored control. The Lublin Poles, existing on the sufferance of the Red Army, were ready to accept the eastern boundary suggested by Moscow, and this added to their unpopularity in London.

Britain and the United States still recognized the London Poles and felt an obligation to return some of these exiles to power. Secretary Stettinius brought to Yalta a State Department proposal for the creation of a new government of national unity, composed of representatives of five political parties, including the Communists. The Peasant Party was still considered by the Americans to be the strongest of the parties and its leader Mikolajczyk was designated for a major role in the new government. Other "moderate Poles," meaning the least anti-Russian, were also to come from London to take up office. Mikolajczyk had resigned the prime ministership in the London government when his Cabinet had refused to give him any flexibility in his effort to negotiate the eastern boundary with Stalin. The American proposal also called for the new government to hold "free elections" when conditions permitted.

Churchill supported Roosevelt and rejected the claim of the Lublin Poles—the Polish Poles, as Stalin called them—to represent the people of that country. British intelligence reported that the Lublin government did not represent more than a third of the Polish people. Who represented the Polish people after five years of war and occupation was difficult to estimate, and the London exiles who fled in 1939 may have spoken for no larger segment than those the Russians selected. As Roosevelt said to Stalin in a moment of frankness, "There hasn't really been any Polish government since 1939." The "free elections" proposed by the United States were also not likely to produce a genuinely representative government in a country that had little experience with this institution. As Stalin reminded his Allies, the de Gaulle regime had been fully recognized and given power without elections. He was unwilling to permit his hand-picked Poles, already established in Warsaw, to be replaced by the London exiles, nor was he willing to trust to an electoral process to return a government that would serve Russian interests in an area of such strategic importance.

Roosevelt and Churchill struggled through most of the eight plenary sessions to break the Russian position. The Western leaders wanted to establish some formula for the new Polish regime that would give it enough pro-Western Poles to counter successfully the Communists and Communist sympathizers who would come from the Lublin government. At a minimum they needed a statement that would enable them to return to Washington and London and assure their constituents that they had begun to create an independent Poland. It was, as Roosevelt said, largely a question of finding the right words. Molotov was willing to have some London Poles added to the Lublin government, but Eden pressed for a completely fresh start. The final wording called for the Lublin regime to be "reorganized on a broader democratic basis." The Russians assumed that this would not mean a change in the basic orientation of the regime that they had created, while Roosevelt and Churchill could hope that the process of reorganization would leave Moscow's selections in a minority.

"Free and unfettered elections" were to be held by the reorganized government, but it was also agreed that these elections could not be completely free. At Molotov's suggestion, the right to take part in the elections was to be limited to "all democratic and anti-Nazi parties," a qualification that Churchill and Roosevelt did not object to, unwilling to defend the right of pro-Nazi elements to return to power by means of the ballot box. This gave those in power a device to exclude rightist and anti-Communist parties from the polls, sometimes with justification, sometimes by stretching terms which had little meaning in Poland's brief modern political history. Roosevelt was not unaware of the likelihood that Poland would now be established within the Soviet orbit. When Admiral William Leahy pointed out to him the elasticity of the wording in the Polish agreement, the President said, "it's the best I can do for Poland at this time."

Rival governments were also disputing for the control of Yugoslavia. A royalist government in exile, headed by King Peter, had been supported by Britain, but by the time of Teheran Churchill decided that Marshal Josip Broz Tito's guerrilla forces were too strong to ignore. In December of 1944 he brought about an accord between Tito and the Prime Minister of the government in exile, intended to create a regency. Elections were to be held within

COMMUNIQUÉ ON THE POLISH PROVISIONAL
GOVERNMENT

A new situation has been created in Poland as a result of her complete liberation by the Red Army. This calls for the establishment of a Polish Provisional Government which can be more broadly based than was possible before the recent liberation of the Western part of Poland. The Provisional Government which is now functioning in Poland should therefore be reorganised on a broader democratic basis with the inclusion of democratic leaders from Poland itself and from Poles abroad. This new Government should then be called the Polish Provisional Government of National Unity.

M. Molotov, Mr. Harriman and Sir A. Clark Kerr are authorised as a commission to consult in the first instance in Moscow with members of the present Provisional Government and with other Polish democratic leaders from within Poland and from abroad, with a view to the reorganisation of the present Government along the above lines. This Polish Provisional Government of National Unity shall be pledged to the holding of free and unfettered elections as soon as possible on the basis of universal suffrage and secret ballot. In these elections all democratic and anti-Nazi parties shall have the right to take part and to put forward candidates.

When a Polish Provisional Government of National Unity has been properly formed in conformity with the above, the Government of the U.S.S.R., which now maintains diplomatic relations with the present Provisional Government of Poland, and the Government of the United Kingdom and the Government of the U.S.A. will establish diplomatic relations with the new Polish Provisional Government of National Unity, and will exchange Ambassadors by whose reports the respective Governments will be kept informed about the situation in Poland.

---

three months after the liberation of Yugoslavia, but no parties or individuals who had collaborated with the Germans were to be allowed to vote or be elected.

A State Department briefing paper had been prepared for Roosevelt at Yalta which warned him that Tito intended to establish "a thoroughly totalitarian regime" and that the accord sponsored by Churchill gave him full legal status. The President was also reminded that Serbian-Americans had already sponsored two Congressional inquiries in respect to executions and property confiscations under Tito's rule. Protests could also be expected, the State Department predicted, from "the large Croatian and Slovenian population" in the United States and, perhaps, from Roman Catholic elements in general. But, as in the case of Poland, the President could do little to satisfy the interests of what the State Department assumed were important voting blocs. With Churchill and Stalin he did "recommend" to Tito and Prime Minister Ivan Subasic of the government in exile that the new legislative assembly include members from the prewar non-Socialist parliament who had not collaborated with the Germans. It was also recommended that Tito's government's actions be subject to subsequent ratification by a constituent assembly. The restoration of a monarchy seemed most unlikely as did the implementation of the President's earlier views that Yugoslavia could not continue as one state.

The almost tacit acceptance of the beginnings of a new Russian orbit in Eastern Europe was in strong contrast to the Declaration on Liberated Europe issued at Yalta. Drafted by the State Department, it was an effort to continue Hull's program of committing the three powers to some broad statement of principles and to reaffirm the Atlantic Charter. Churchill said at Yalta that the Charter was "not a law, but a star," and the same might have been said of the Declaration. The Russians had no objections to describing a star, and Churchill did not later consider the statement important enough to mention in his memoirs. The American draft was, consequently, accepted intact except for a decision to include an invitation to the French government to associate itself with the Declaration.

In two geographic areas outside of Europe where conflicts of interest were to disturb the postwar relationship of the Allies, an effort was made to reach some settlement at Yalta, but the issues were postponed. Iran or Persia had become an important military base, serving as a transportation link between the Persian Gulf and

DECLARATION ON LIBERATED EUROPE

The Premier of the Union of Soviet Socialist Republics, the Prime Minister of the United Kingdom and the President of the United States of America have consulted with each other in the common interests of the peoples of their countries and those of liberated Europe. They jointly declare their mutual agreement to concert during the temporary period of instability in liberated Europe the policies of their three governments in assisting the peoples liberated from the domination of Nazi Germany and the peoples of the former Axis satellite states of Europe to solve by democratic means their pressing political and economic problems.

The establishment of order in Europe and the re-building of national economic life must be achieved by processes which will enable the liberated peoples to destroy the last vestiges of Nazism and Fascism and to create democratic institutions of their own choice. This is a principle of the Atlantic Charter—the right of all peoples to choose the form of government under which they will live—the restoration of sovereign rights and self-government to those peoples who have been forcibly deprived of them by the aggressor nations.

To foster the conditions in which the liberated peoples may exercise these rights, the three governments will jointly assist the people and any European liberated state or former Axis satellite state in Europe where in their judgment conditions require (a) to establish conditions of internal peace; (b) to carry out emergency measures for the relief of distressed peoples; (c) to form interim governmental authorities broadly representative of all democratic elements in the population and pledged to the earliest possible establishment through free elections of governments responsive to the will of the people; and (d) to facilitate where necessary the holding of such elections.

The three governments will consult the other United Nations and provisional authorities or other governments in Europe when matters of direct interest to them are under consideration.

When, in the opinion of the three governments, conditions in any European liberated state or any former Axis satellite state in Europe make such action necessary, they will immediately consult together on the measures necessary to discharge the joint responsibilities set forth in this declaration.

By this declaration we reaffirm our faith in the principles of the Atlantic Charter, our pledge in the Declaration by the United Nations, and our determination to build in co-operation with other peace-loving nations world order under law, dedicated to peace, security, freedom and general well-being of all mankind.

In issuing this declaration, the Three Powers express the hope that the Provisional Government of the French Republic may be associated with them in the procedure suggested.

the Soviet border, and occupied by Russian, British, and American troops. The area had long been a source of Russo-British conflict, only settled in 1907 by the delimitation and recognition of their respective zones of interest. During the first decades of the Soviet Union, Russian influence had become minimal. The British were afraid that the wartime presence might be used to re-establish a Russian role and to challenge British dominance in oil concessions. American oil companies also developed an interest in Iranian resources, introducing another national interest. As a result of his visit for the Teheran conference, Roosevelt decided that the United States ought to play an active part in aiding the development of Iran in the postwar world. American technical skill, he believed, could develop the water and agricultural resources of this area as an example of "unselfish American policy."

At Teheran the three powers had signed a declaration that expressed their desire to maintain Iranian sovereignty and their intention of providing economic assistance at the end of the war. When in early 1944 the Russians pressed for oil concessions in northern Iran, concessions that were refused them, the British and Americans began to fear Soviet penetration. Eden, helped by Stettinius at Yalta, sought a pact by which all powers would schedule the withdrawal of their troops when the war ended. At the same time the Russians were assured that no obstacles would be placed in the way of their acquisition of oil concessions. Molotov refused to be drawn into this commitment that went beyond the Teheran declaration. The communiqué subsequently mentioned only that the foreign ministers had "exchanged views."

The second area was Turkey and the Straits. Since the Turks had resisted Allied efforts to enlist them in the war, the Russians expected they would have no defenders among the victors. At Moscow in October of 1944, Stalin asked for a modification of the 1936 Montreux Convention to permit free passage for Soviet warships. Churchill stated his agreement in principle, leaving it to the Russians to make detailed proposals. At Yalta the State Department, supported by the Navy Department, opposed a change of regime and held that "by and large Turkey has been a

good custodian of the Straits." Internationalization of this waterway was also opposed, possibly because it might suggest similar
treatment for the Panama Canal and Suez. Roosevelt was advised
before Yalta to oppose any major changes in the Montreux
Convention and to accept minor changes only after they had been
considered by the Navy and War departments. Since the United
States had not been a member of the 1936 agreement, this active
interest in the eastern Mediterranean indicated a radical expansion
of the concept of American interests. Roosevelt, however, took no
heed of this briefing paper. Stettinius was permitted to accept a
protocol by which the foreign ministers would consider the Soviet
proposals for changes and report to their government.

One territorial arrangement was made directly between
Roosevelt and Stalin, without informing the British. It produced
what Eden later considered "a discreditable by-product of the
Conference." This was the setting of the terms by which the Soviet
Union was to enter the war against Japan. The American Joint
Chiefs of Staff were very anxious to be assured of Soviet action,
assuming that the defeat of Japan was many months and possibly
years away. Russian troops, attacking the Japanese in China, could
shorten the war and save many American lives. Any price the
Soviet Union asked for participation seemed suitable, particularly
if it meant territorial concessions to areas at that time in control of
Japan. Roosevelt deferred to military opinion in this matter and
was prepared to make the kind of concessions he would have been
unwilling to make in Europe.

As early as December of 1944, Stalin outlined to Ambassador
Harriman the Russian interests in Asia. Southern Sakhalin, lost to
Japan in 1905, was to be returned. The Kurile Islands, a chain
stretching northward from Hokkaido to the Kamchatka Peninsula, were another Russian objective. The Tsarist rights once held
in Manchuria were a third aspiration: specifically the leasing of the
Chinese Eastern railroad, and leases on Dairen and Port Arthur.

At Yalta, in a private meeting with Roosevelt, attended only
by Harriman and Charles Bohlen from the American delegation,
Stalin again stated his specific objectives. Roosevelt said that he

had no objection to the retrocession of southern Sakhalin and to the acquisition of the Kuriles, but he preferred that Dairen be made a free port under some form of international control. Soviet interest in preserving the *status quo* of Outer Mongolia was also acceptable, but Roosevelt said that arrangements dealing with China must have the concurrence of Chiang Kai-shek. On this basis the secret protocol was drafted, signed, and known only to the President's closest advisers. When Secretary Stettinius asked the President about the Far Eastern discussions, he was told that they dealt primarily with military matters. Extreme secrecy was due in part to the concern of the Soviet Union that Japan receive no hint of this pact and attack Siberia before the end of the European War. Churchill signed the protocol, but regarded it as "an American affair."

The agreements in respect to Asia were to become for many critics the worst mistake made at Yalta. As time demonstrated, the American military estimates that the Japanese would continue the war for eighteen months after the defeat of Germany were overly pessimistic. The Joint Chiefs of Staff had given little or no weight to the effect of the atomic bomb, which they had been advised would be ready for use by the first of August. Japanese peace feelers, made through Sweden as early as September of 1944, by members of the Japanese Cabinet were dismissed as evidence of Japan's readiness to make peace. Reports of intelligence specialists on evidences of defeatism among Japanese soldiers were also underevaluated.

Two decades after Yalta, however, the political effects of the concessions in contributing to Soviet power in Asia seemed negligible. The Russians had withdrawn from Manchuria in deference to the interests of the Chinese People's Republic and faced a hostile rival for world Communist leadership. The acquisitions from Japan only added an obstacle to Russo-Japanese friendship and contributed little, if anything, to Soviet strength in the Pacific.

The character of the new international organization was another important item on the Yalta agenda. In August and September of 1944, discussions had taken place on the Dumbarton

Agreement

The leaders of the three Great Powers—the Soviet Union, the United States of America and Great Britain—have agreed that in two or three months after Germany has surrendered and the war in Europe has terminated the Soviet Union shall enter into the war against Japan on the side of the Allies on condition that:

1. The *status quo* in Outer-Mongolia (The Mongolian People's Republic) shall be preserved;

2. The former rights of Russia violated by the treacherous attack of Japan in 1904 shall be restored, viz:

(*a*) the southern part of Sakhalin as well as all the islands adjacent to it shall be returned to the Soviet Union,

(*b*) the commercial port of Dairen shall be internationalized, the preeminent interests of the Soviet Union in this port being safeguarded and the lease of Port Arthur as a naval base of the USSR restored,

(*c*) the Chinese-Eastern Railroad and the South-Manchurian Railroad which provides an outlet to Dairen shall be jointly operated by the establishment of a joint Soviet-Chinese Company it being understood that the preeminent interests of the Soviet Union shall be safeguarded and that China shall retain full sovereignty in Manchuria;

3. The Kuril islands shall be handed over to the Soviet Union.

It is understood, that the agreement concerning Outer-Mongolia and the ports and railroads referred to above will require concurrence of Generalissimo Chiang Kai-Shek. The President will take measures in order to obtain this concurrence on advice from Marshal Stalin.

The Heads of the three Great Powers have agreed that these claims of the Soviet Union shall be unquestionably fulfilled after Japan has been defeated.

For its part the Soviet Union expresses its readiness to conclude with the National Government of China a pact of friendship and alliance between the USSR and China in order to render assistance to China with its armed forces for the purpose of liberating China from the Japanese yoke.

J. STALIN   И. Сталин
FRANKLIN D. ROOSEVELT
WINSTON S. CHURCHILL

February 11, 1954.

Oaks estate in Washington in which the Allied powers had agreed on the title "United Nations." The Four Policemen, joined by France, were to have permanent membership in a Security Council to which six small powers were to be elected for a two-year term. The United States tried to secure a permanent seat for the largest Latin-American nation, Brazil, but it was opposed by both Britain and the Soviet Union. Agreement was reached on the principle that the Security Council would only act on the basis of the unity of the big powers and that each had the power to veto actions that it opposed.

The Soviet delegation to Dumbarton Oaks had taken two positions at odds with the United States and Britain. The first was Soviet unwillingness to accept the rule that a major power, when party to a dispute coming before the Council, would not be able to exercise a veto to prevent consideration of this case. The British argued that the smaller powers would be unwilling to accept an organization in which the veto power of the major states was so inclusive. The second Soviet stand was to claim, as the revised Soviet constitution provided, that each of the sixteen Soviet republics was free to conduct foreign relations and should be voting members of the United Nations. In this way the Russians believed they would be assured of a bloc of votes in the General Assembly to counter the Anglo-American bloc that was expected to include the British Dominions and many of the Latin-American states. The audacity of this proposal was a shock to the American delegates and threatened to block progress on establishing the new organization. Plans had been made to hold the conference to write the Charter in the spring of 1945, but the Russians were unwilling to attend until these two issues were resolved.

Roosevelt was very anxious at Yalta to overcome these obstacles to what was to become the San Francisco Conference. He made a strong argument that the suspension of the veto would in no way prevent a major power from stopping the Security Council from acting against it. A Soviet concession was made that gave the Security Council the right to make decisions on procedural matters with seven out of the eleven votes. Stalin also agreed to cut the

Russian votes from sixteen down to three. Churchill did not see how this claim could be rejected in view of the votes of the British Dominions, including that assigned India, which was not yet a sovereign state. Consequently, the Ukrainian and Byelorussian Socialist republics were admitted to United Nations membership. This decision was strongly criticized in the United States when it became known, but the expansion of Assembly membership soon made these two additional Soviet votes of no consequence. Stalin did make it easier for Roosevelt by dropping his request for a vote for Lithuania as a Soviet Republic, while the United States still recognized the prewar Lithuanian government in exile.

Without debate it was decided to counter the heritage of American distrust in the League of Nations by creating the new organization in the United States. The date was set for late April, and after a survey of available cities, Roosevelt accepted Stettinius' suggestion for San Francisco.

Roosevelt's last venture at Yalta was to tackle the problem of colonialism with his program for territorial trusteeships. He received, however, rough handling from Churchill, who saw the whole idea as an effort to dismantle the British Empire. "We can always say to the United States, will you take over a mandate for Ethiopia?" he wrote Eden in November of 1944, certain that Americans would then "recoil most meekly and with great rapidity" from their desire to establish trusteeships. (As a sovereign state, Ethiopia had never been considered in the trusteeship category, of course, but may have been the Prime Minister's whimsical selection for the most difficult ward.)

Roosevelt was not discouraged by any evidence that Churchill would be difficult. He believed that the trusteeship question had to be settled since the League of Nations could not be liquidated without some disposition of the system of mandates established in 1919 to handle the colonies of the defeated powers. There had also been some public criticism in the United States of the failure to provide for trusteeships in the Dumbarton agreements. When the American proposal was read at Yalta, Churchill, according to Stettinius, "exploded." He would not accept a single word in the

American draft and said that under no circumstances would he consent to "forty or fifty nations thrusting interfering fingers into the life's existence of the British Empire." Every scrap of territory under the British flag was immune. Stettinius finally made it clear that there was no intention of touching British possessions, and when the Prime Minister calmed down a secret protocol was finally signed.

PROTOCOL ON TERRITORIAL TRUSTEESHIPS

It was agreed that the five Nations which will have permanent seats on the Security Council should consult each other prior to the United Nations Conference on the question of territorial trusteeship.

The acceptance of this recommendation is subject to its being made clear that territorial trusteeship will only apply to (*a*) existing mandates of the League of Nations; (*b*) territories detached from the enemy as a result of the present war; (*c*) any other territory which might voluntarily be placed under trusteeship; and (*d*) no discussion of actual territories is contemplated at the forthcoming United Nations Conference or in the preliminary consultations, and it will be a matter for subsequent agreement which territories within the above categories will be placed under trusteeship.

Some of the conference members felt that more time should be taken to clarify some of the pending issues, but the President was insistent on his leaving date. He had, he said, to meet the "Three Kings," the monarchs of Egypt, Ethiopia, and Saudi Arabia, on his way home. This was not a conference of any major political importance, and Hopkins felt that the President was anxious to attend it only to enjoy the colorful panoply of these sovereigns.

When he returned to Washington the President spoke to Congress on March 1, his physical weakness now requiring him to remain seated during the address. He presented the results of Yalta in a most favorable light. The Polish boundaries, he admitted, were "frankly a compromise" with which he did not completely agree. But he said that as compensation for losses to the Soviet Union the Poles would get "quite a slice of what now is called Germany." As for the two Polish governments, he said that country needed an *ad interim* regime "in the worst way" and the reorganized Lublin government would fill the need. In his conclusion he returned to the Wilsonian dream and said that the Crimean Conference "ought to spell the end of the system of unilateral action, the exclusive alliances, the spheres of influence, the balances of power, and the other expedients that have been tried for centuries—and have always failed."

Prime Minister Churchill was less optimistic in his address to Parliament. The Polish settlement, he admitted, opened the way, if the Russians so intended, to make Poland a Communist vassal. But he refused to speculate on Soviet intentions; his policy was clear: "While the war is on we will give aid to anyone who can kill a Hun." After the war, Britain would look to solutions by means of democratic elections. He also told Parliament of the success of the British Army in putting down the Communist opposition in Greece and installing a pro-British government. Although the October 1944 arrangement by which Stalin agreed to give Britain a free hand in Greece was still secret, the Prime Minister may have been hinting to Parliament that he had also received acceptance of British interests. Stalin had reassured him at Yalta that no questions would be raised about Greece.

In the United States, the word "Yalta" was to become like "Munich" for the Russians, a pejorative word that connoted betrayal. Roosevelt was charged with failure to defend the interests of the United States and its Polish and Chinese friends. The President's personal role at this conference can be easily faulted. The deteriorating state of his health made it unwise for him to attempt major negotiations, which required intellectual and physical stamina. But it is also difficult to make a case for the possibility of completely satisfying American interests in this exchange with the Soviet Union and Britain. Bargains are rare in international politics, and national aspirations are frequently overpriced. What those Americans who attacked Yalta wanted would have cost more than the American public was willing to pay. Some goals, such as the achievement of bonafide constitutional regimes in Eastern Europe, based on Anglo-American type elections, may have been impossible to achieve at any price without long years of preparation.

9

Potsdam and the Cold War Mood

President Roosevelt's death on April 12, 1945, came at a time of growing turbulence in the relations of the Western Allies with Moscow. In Washington the hopes for the creation of a government in Warsaw acceptable to Polish-American opinion were dying. The American and British ambassadors to Moscow, charged with the reorganization of the Lublin regime in co-operation with Molotov, found their efforts futile. The Russians were unwilling to approve most of the Polish leaders nominated by London and Washington and were determined that the additional cabinet members coming from London would have no real power. Sixteen of the leaders of the Polish underground, invited to Moscow for discussions, were arrested and tried for subversive activities. One of the last messages sent to Stalin over Roosevelt's name was a lengthy indictment of the Soviet treatment of the Yalta protocol on Poland.

Rumania became another area of dispute as the United States saw the principles of the Declaration on Liberated Europe disregarded. The Russians intervened in Bucharest to oust an anti-Russian premier and to replace him with their own selection. Churchill felt constrained to withhold his complaint since Rumania had been assigned 90 percent to the Soviet Union by the

October 1944 agreement. The United States felt in no way constrained by this demarcation of spheres, which the British said was only a temporary arrangement. Some State Department officials believed that Soviet intervention in Rumania foreshadowed Soviet control of all of Eastern Europe.

Western suspicion of the intentions of the Kremlin was matched by Stalin's distrust of his allies. German troops, fearful of their treatment by the Russians, were putting up a vigorous fight on the Eastern Front while expressing a willingness to surrender on the Western Front. Nazi hopes were still strong for splitting their enemies and making a more favorable peace with Britain and the United States. German contacts, which opened up discussions of the surrender of the German armies in Italy, were made with agents of the Office of Strategic Services in Italy in late February. When the Combined Chiefs of Staff became directly involved in this matter, they informed the Soviet Union, but refused to permit a Russian representative to be present. Stalin then claimed that the surrender talks enabled the Germans to withdraw three divisions from Italy that were thrown against the Russian front. He began to see a general plan to keep Soviet forces engaged, while the Germans permitted the Western Allies to move deeper into Germany. His last communications to Roosevelt on this subject were bitter in their accusations despite the President's efforts to assure him that Russian intelligence sources were wrong about German troop movement.

Other elements added to this friction at the same time that great public hopes were being raised in the United States in connection with the forthcoming San Francisco Conference. The new international organization was to surmount the weaknesses of the League, to be born on American soil, and to have the United States as a charter member. But a chill was produced in the State Department in mid-March when Moscow reported that Foreign Minister Molotov would be unable to attend. This suggested that the Soviet Union was giving little importance to the U.N. At the same time there was embarrassing news that a party of thirty delegates were coming to represent the Soviet republics of the

Ukraine and Byelorussia, although the Yalta decision to give the Soviet Union three votes was not public. Confronted with this news at his last press conference, Roosevelt dismissed its importance by saying that the General Assembly was going to be "an investigatory body only" and would not decide anything. The Russians further embarrassed Washington by insisting that an invitation be given to the Polish government, which was still unrecognized in the West.

President Truman took office ill-prepared for the situation and decisions he faced in foreign affairs. He had not been a member of Roosevelt's inner circle during his months as Vice President and knew little of the policies and programs under consideration. Harry Hopkins, who had been privy to much of Roosevelt's thinking, was ill. Secretary Stettinius was new to his post and of limited stature. The President needed, however, to have sound advice on the many issues that could no longer be evaded or postponed.

The major question was how to deal with the Russians, and on this point Truman had advice from two broad viewpoints. One held, as the President was later to say of himself, that Americans were tired of "babying the Russians." With Hitler's armies collapsing, there was no longer a need to put military matters first; a hard-boiled attitude was now possible in dealing with Moscow. Blunt and strong protests should be made over Soviet actions in Eastern Europe. Lend-Lease supplies should be rationed to secure Moscow's compliance. The San Francisco Conference should be held without the Soviet Union if Stalin demanded too many concessions for participation.

This policy was strongly encouraged by the advice sent across the Atlantic by Prime Minister Churchill. He was now urgently concerned about the imbalance of power that threatened the postwar world on a scale comparable to Napoleonic France at its peak of power. As Russian troops drove deeper into Central Europe, mopping up anti-Russian political opposition behind the lines, Churchill had pressed Roosevelt to take a harder line. In mid-March of 1945 the President said jocularly that the British were now willing for the United States to go to war with the Soviet Union at any time. With Truman in office, Churchill renewed his efforts to stiffen the American position. When American armies overran by more than a hundred miles in some spearheads the line established to divide the Russian and Western occupation zones, Churchill urged that the troops stay in place as a bargaining factor in securing Russian concessions before they withdrew.

Those in the small circle of Americans who knew of the progress being made on producing the first atomic weapons included some who thought of it as power to be displayed in producing better behavior in Moscow. When James Byrnes told the new President about work on the bomb on April 13, Truman's first day in office, he expressed his belief that it "might well put us in a position to dictate our own terms at the end of the war." Truman himself later said in the presence of his secretary Jonathan Daniels, "If it explodes, as I think it will, I'll certainly have a hammer on those boys." Not all the advocates of a get-tough policy were advocating a military showdown; many believed that possession of atomic weapons coupled with a firm and unyielding position would win the respect and friendship of the Russians.

The other wing of American opinion interpreted Russian actions, not as indications of aggressive intent and expansionist appetites, but as the work of a very insecure, war-battered, and suspicious nation. Almost pathological in its concern for security, as some Americans saw the Kremlin, the Soviet leaders could only be dissuaded from a ruthless effort to create a belt of satellite states by being assured that security could also be found in the United Nations. As Russia was outnumbered in the new organization by British and American supporters and remembered its treatment by the League, only time and sympathetic co-operation—it was argued —could produce a co-operative, trusting Soviet Union.

In his first weeks in office, Truman fluctuated between the two viewpoints. On April 23, after listening to his military and political advisors debate policy, Truman concluded that agreements with the Soviet Union had been so far a one-way street. If the Russians did not wish to join in the San Francisco plans, he said, "they could go to hell." In this mood he had his first discussion with Foreign Minister Molotov, who was finally authorized to attend the U.N. conference. The language Truman used on the Russian visitor was very tough; according to the President himself, Molotov closed the interview by saying that he had "never been talked to like that in my life."

But Truman did not act tough in all areas. Early in May, Churchill warned that if the American troops all withdrew after victory to the agreed-upon occupation zones, "the tide of Russian domination" would sweep westward 120 miles, an event he called "one of the most melancholy in history." As the Germans collapsed, Churchill also appealed to Eisenhower to push on to take Prague before it fell into the hands of the Red Army. But the American Commander of the Allied forces refused to try to take Prague for political ends, as he had refused to focus on taking Berlin before the Red Army reached the capital. Truman also resisted Churchill's appeals, and after the German surrender on May 8 the American armies pulled back to the occupation lines set months earlier.

Truman, like Roosevelt, was impressed by the arguments of General George Marshall and other military men for the great need of Soviet participation in the Pacific war. This consideration, along with the arguments of the opponents of a tough policy, was behind his decision to send Hopkins to Moscow and Joseph Davies to London. Both men believed that Russo-American friendship was possible and essential; both were opposed to the Cold War outlook expressed by the other wing of American opinion. Davies returned to Washington early in June, shocked by Churchill's vehemence in his attacks on the Soviet Union, and without having convinced the Prime Minister that his tough policies would only harden the Russian attitude toward its allies.

The Hopkins-Stalin talks, attended by Ambassador Harriman, began on May 26 and continued for more than a week. They were the fullest, frankest, and possibly the friendliest Russo-American exchange to take place before the Cold War mood settled down over both capitals. Stalin heard Hopkins go through the agenda of American grievances and in turn presented his complaints against Britain and the United States. Little was agreed upon besides the need for a peace conference in Germany, but the way seemed open for further settlements.

When the meetings closed, Poland still remained the major area of disagreement. Harriman reported to Truman:

> I am afraid that Stalin does not and never will fully understand our interest in a free Poland as a matter of principle. He is a realist in all his actions, and it is hard for him to appreciate our faith in abstract principles. It is difficult for him to understand why we should want to interfere with Soviet policy in a country like Poland, which he considers so important to Russia's security, unless we have some ulterior motive.

Repeatedly Stalin reverted to the precedent of the *cordon sanitaire,* accusing the British of trying to recreate that political wall by reinstating the anti-Russian, London Poles in power.

Stalin also complained about the formation of the United Nations. He charged the United States with breaking its pledge in pressing for the admission of the Argentine government as a charter member. The Buenos Aires government had been sympathetic to Nazi Germany and unwilling to join in the Allied war effort. The United States did reverse its position in supporting United Nations membership because of Washington's interest in maintaining unity with the other Latin-American states that favored Argentine admission. The decision had also been criticized in America. Stettinius defended it by saying that the United States in supporting membership did not give blanket endorsement to the policies of the Argentine government. The Latin-American nations, however, insisted on Argentine membership when they learned of the extra two Assembly votes given the Soviet Union.

The decision to include France on the Reparations Commission was another Russian grievance. Russia considered that a defeated nation that had contributed little to the war effort did not deserve an important role in sharing the resources of Germany. The reluctance of the Allies to agree on a figure for German reparations added to Soviet suspicions. Stalin was also piqued by the apparent unwillingness of Britain and the United States to begin reparations by sharing the captured German Navy and merchant marine on the suggested one-third basis.

In listening to Stalin's array of complaints, Hopkins did secure an important concession in respect to the U.N. Charter. On two important paragraphs the Russians were refusing to accept the proposed wording, one giving freedom to the Assembly to make recommendations, and the other limiting the veto power of the Security Council members. Hopkins' successful intercession removed the last obstacles to completing the Charter on the basis of the Dumbarton Oaks drafts. It was unanimously adopted by the delegates of the fifty countries on July 25, 1945 and proclaimed by President Truman as the "solid structure upon which we can build a better world." The Senate avoided the lengthy debates and decisions to amend, which had characterized the case of the League of Nations, and ratified American membership by a 61–2 vote on July 28.

The new organization began in a far more complex form than Roosevelt had envisaged. The dominant role of his Four Policemen was considerably weakened by broadening the membership of the Security Council to eleven. The Assembly was given a larger role than he seems to have projected. And the readiness of the United States to accept a part in a new experiment was far greater than Roosevelt and many of the supporters of the United Nations had hoped.

One favorite Roosevelt scheme was very much diluted, in good part as a result of a shift in American policy. This was the creation of a Trusteeship Council. The wording of this section of the Charter posed no threat to the existing colonial system except for that of Italy and Japan. Even these colonies were not to be put under genuine international control. The United States Navy put forth a strong claim for the Japanese islands of Micronesia as essential for national security. The Navy was opposed to any interference by representatives of the new international organization. The State Department initially opposed this deviation from the original intent of the trusteeship concept and fought the Navy proposal. Roosevelt failed to decide between the contestants, and on his death the Navy triumphed with the argument of national security. A provision was included in the trusteeship chapter of the Charter for "strategic areas" in which the trustee was virtually given a free hand. A Soviet and Chinese proposal to insert a statement that independence was the ultimate objective for the trust territories was opposed by Britain and France. The United States supported the two older colonial powers, and the final draft included only the goal of "progressive development towards self-government."

Another qualification in the scope of the U.N. was made at the behest of the United States and the Latin-American nations. This provided for regional security pacts and made possible the inter-American security organization that was considered a modernized form of the Monroe Doctrine. Provision for regional organizations also opened the way in 1949 for the North Atlantic Treaty Organization and the Soviet-sponsored Warsaw pact. Universality as a goal, and American abhorrence for spheres of influence had not ended special regional interests.

The San Francisco Conference closed on June 25, and shortly afterwards President Truman left for Berlin to preside at the Potsdam Conference. It was "a chore," as he wrote to his mother, and he had to take his "tuxedo, tails . . . preacher coat, high hat, low hat and hard hat." Thus equipped, he opened the first plenary meeting of the Big Three at the Cecilienhof Palace on July 17. There were thirteen plenary sessions and eleven formal meetings of the foreign ministers. It was the last wartime meeting of the Big Three and the last time the heads of the three countries were to meet until 1955, when Eden as Prime Minister sat down with President Eisenhower and Premier Bulganin in Geneva, Switzerland.

President Truman brought with him his new Secretary of State James Byrnes, leaving Stettinius behind in Washington as the first delegate to the United Nations Security Council. Harry Hopkins was too ill to travel, and the President relied heavily on career officers in the Department of State along with his Joint Chiefs of Staff and their aides. Churchill brought with him not only Eden but his deputy Clement Attlee, head of the Labour Party. When Churchill's Conservative Party was defeated at the polls while the conference was in session, Attlee returned to take Churchill's seat on July 28, while Ernest Bevin became the new Foreign Minister. Stalin and Molotov consequently had the experience of dealing with a new set of American and British representatives, although in both cases the professional staffs provided the new leaders with some continuity in policies.

When the Conference opened, the Americans made clear that they were no longer in favor of a peace conference on the scale of Versailles, the final framing of the postwar world for which Roosevelt had deferred so many difficult tasks. The number of nations that would want to attend would be too great, the discussions so lengthy and the great power decisions so likely to be challenged, that the Americans felt that such a formal gathering should be avoided. The British and the Russians had also realized how much more difficult the already difficult issues would become when new sets of national interests were introduced. Both were quick to agree to the American suggestion for an alternate procedure, the establishment of a Council of Foreign Ministers to prepare the peace treaties for signatures and ratification. In some instances small conferences could then be called for signatures of the states chiefly concerned. France and China were to be made members of the Council along with the Big Three. The Russians objected to giving China a voice in European affairs and were also reluctant to give France a part in drafting the peace treaties with the German satellites in Eastern Europe. With these exceptions agreed to, the new Council was established, a major procedural achievement of Potsdam.

For almost two years after Potsdam closed, the Council struggled and finally produced four peace treaties for Italy, Rumania, Hungary, and Bulgaria. These were ratified by the United States Senate in June of 1947 and came into force the following September. The Council, without French and American representatives, completed the Finnish treaty in February of 1947, incorporating the territorial concessions of the Soviet armistice of 1944. Its major task, the creation of a treaty with Germany, the Council failed to achieve as the divisions of the Cold War proved too great for the skill of the ministers in finding compromises. Its work was, nevertheless, a demonstration of the value of more conventional diplomatic procedures. Unlike the Big Three with their disregard for agenda and their unwillingness, sometimes for lack of time, to pursue the wearisome task of finding suitable middle ways and careful wordings, the ministers with their professional staffs were able to hold to the traditional diplomacy's path.

With the supplementary treaties postponed, the Big Three devoted much of the time at Potsdam to the central matter of the treatment of defeated Germany. For a variety of reasons dismemberment of Germany, generally assumed during the war years, no longer was proposed. The Americans and British seem to have reached this view first, with Churchill reluctantly giving up the idea of severing Prussia from the Reich. Stalin by early May also expressed in public the Soviet opposition to the dissection of Germany, and by tacit agreement the earlier proposals were not taken up at Potsdam. The furthest the Conference was willing to go was to state that the administration of Germany was to be "directed toward the decentralization of the political structure."

The British and Americans had also changed their views greatly on the subject of reparations. Any major program of dismantling German industry posed many practical problems previously given little consideration. The Morgenthau Plan and other proposals for severe economic measures had not considered how much of the productive structure would be destroyed by bombing and ground battle. Unless the Germans were fed, and the labor force given employment, social and political chaos would result, creating a great burden for the Occupation authorities. The problem of feeding alone was already drawing heavily on Western resources, and a drastic program of reparations would require even greater food importations to keep the Germans alive. The task of creating a new, democratic Germany in the midst of rubble and homeless refugees seemed to be difficult enough without eliminating large segments of industry.

Neither the Americans nor the British in 1945 were ready to restore Germany to full prosperity. The directive of the Joint Chiefs, JCS 1067, which guided early occupation policy in the American zone, called for a German standard of living no higher than in neighboring United Nations. Since the Germans seemed better fed and clothed at the war's end than the victorious British, due to the exploitation of the occupied territories, this meant a lowering of the German living standard. But it was also acknowledged by some Americans that European prosperity before the war was closely intertwined with the German economy; even Britain had looked to the Germans as their second-best customers and second major source of supplies. It was self-defeating, therefore, to weaken the German economy until it was a drag on the victors. American and British economic policy fell, therefore, between the extremes urged by Morgenthau and his supporters and the other extreme of completely restoring German well-being.

The Soviet Union with its own devastated industry to restore was little concerned about German difficulties and possible political disorders. The Red Army set about to strip the Reich of whatever seemed useful in speeding the recovery of the Soviet Union, with little concern for its effect on the defeated. Since the Big Three had so frequently endorsed harsh treatment of the Germans, it was difficult for the British or Americans to make a principled protest against Russian actions. Molotov was also anxious to reach agreement on the total reparations, and repeatedly raised at Potsdam the figure of $20 billion set at Yalta as the basis of discussion. The Reparations Commission had agreed before Potsdam on a division that would give 56 percent of the total exacted from Germany to the Soviet Union and 22 percent each to Britain and the United States. Other national claims, such as those of Poland and France, were to be satisfied by the Big Three out of their own portions.

The British and Americans were unwilling to set any figure

for total reparations, pleading the difficulties in estimating what was available and of evaluating the industrial equipment and factories to be dismantled and carted away. After almost reaching an impasse, despite the Soviet willingness to cut the $20 billion figure, agreement was reached on permitting each power to take its reparations from its own occupation zone. Since the British and American zones included the most highly industrialized areas of Germany, the Soviet Union was to receive 10 percent from this area and another 15 percent in exchange for an equivalent value of raw materials and foods from the predominantly agricultural Soviet zone.

With this decision on zonal reparations, there was tacit acceptance that joint occupation policies would be minimal. The Allied Control Commission, which included the French, became a body of limited power except for Berlin, where its power also waned.

By the close of the Potsdam Conference on August 2, it was clear that the Big Three agreed on little other than that Germany should be prevented from launching new wars of aggression. Whether this was to be accomplished by taking away the means of aggression, removing the desire to aggress or making certain that aggression would not pay, was subject to disagreement both as to which of these avenues to concentrate upon and the best means to achieve the end. The Soviet Union had the most consistent approach, believing that Germany must not only be deprived of war industries, but more importantly, drastically reformed. This reformation for Marxists meant a radical change of the socioeconomic structure to deprive the former ruling class of power. Even though the Russians had initially expressed some belief that Communism was too good a system for the hated Germans—Stalin said that Communism would fit Germany as a saddle fitted a cow—they nevertheless began socializing the economy of their zone and putting German Communists in positions of power.

The Americans, and to a lesser extent the British, saw no need for a redistribution of property in their zones. It was deemed sufficient to introduce democratic political institutions into the existing socioeconomic structure and to reinforce them with a program of education. As a result the American and British zones, joined in 1947, soon took on a different character from the Russian zone and the zonal boundaries acquired a political nature that had not been foreseen.

The major measure of de-Nazification on which the Big Three agreed was the holding of trials of German war criminals to bring them to "swift and sure justice." Conducted at Nuremberg, these unusual proceedings led to the conviction of nineteen high Nazi leaders by their conclusion in October of 1946. In both the United States and Britain, they were strongly criticized as being *ex post facto,* trying men for violating nonexistent laws, and thus abusing the judicial process.

On one question, Germany's future borders, the Potsdam conferees deferred decisions to the peace conference that was never to meet. The Polish-German border established by the Russians was accepted only to the extent that the area acquired by Warsaw was recognized as being temporarily under the administration of the Polish government. Any transfer of German population from this area, as well as from Czechoslovakia and Hungary, was to be effected in "an orderly and humane manner" according to the final protocol. Recognition of Polish administration was a concession made by the British and Americans for Soviet willingness to accept the zonal reparations plan, a "package deal" devised by Secretary Byrnes. The Poles had already occupied the area with Soviet permission; London and Washington recognized a *de facto* situation while reaffirming with the Russians "that the final delimitation of the western frontier of Poland should await the peace settlement." Soviet acquisition of a segment of East Prussia, including Königsberg, was accepted in principle with a declaration by the President and British Prime Minister that they would support the Soviet proposal "at the forthcoming peace settlement."

Outside of the German questions, the Big Three also had difficulty in reaching any comprehensive agreements. President Truman surprised his Allies by claiming that all wars in the past two centuries had originated in Central Europe. The way to prevent this, he urged, would be to internationalize the Rhine, the Danube, and the Dardanelles. This radical suggestion touched on too many formidable national interests to be seriously considered. To avoid any debate, Truman's ideas were referred to the Council of Foreign Ministers for study and discussion at a later date.

Stalin was still interested in some major changes in the control of the Straits and in the abrogation of the 1936 Montreux Convention. Churchill agreed that modifications should be made in the Convention to give the Soviet Navy free access to the Mediterranean, but he was also opposed to giving the Russians any part in controlling this strategic waterway. The final protocol stated agreement on the revision of the Montreux Convention because it failed to meet present-day conditions, but proposed as the next step direct conversations with the Turkish government. After the Potsdam Conference closed, the United States did propose changes to the Turks to give freer access to the ships of the Red Fleet. The Russians wanted to go further. They asked for a part in the defense of the Straits, which would have meant Soviet bases. They also asked the Turks to return the territory of Kars and Ardahan in Armenia. Acquired as a result of the Russo-Turkish war of 1877–78, this mountainous region was recovered by the Turks at a time of Russian weakness in 1921.

Turkey refused to make any concessions to the Soviet Union. When Soviet pressures persisted, the United States radically extended the sphere of its interests, committing itself to the defense of Turkish boundaries and Turkish control of the Straits. The Truman Doctrine, proclaimed in March of 1947, followed by the Greek-Turkish aid program, led to the incorporation of Turkey in the North Atlantic Treaty Organization. Stalin thus failed to achieve the power over the Straits promised the Tsar by Britain and France in 1915, while the United States took up Britain's historic interest in containing Russian power in the Middle East and the eastern Mediterranean.

The most important event which took place during the Potsdam Conference was never discussed openly by the Big Three. On July 16, as he waited for the Conference to begin, Truman received word of the successful explosion on that day of the first atomic weapon at Alamogordo, New Mexico. A few days later he received a full report of the test and was told that the new weapon had far greater destructive power than had been expected. Preparations were immediately made and approved by the President for the dropping of the first bombs on Japanese cities. Secretary of War Stimson noted that Truman said that the existence of the new weapon gave him "an entirely new feeling of confidence." Churchill noted the change in the President's attitude at the conference; the bomb, as he saw it, had produced a Truman who stood up to the Russians in a new and decisive manner.

Churchill was full informed of the new developments, but Stalin only received mention of its existence in a brief aside. Whether the Soviet Premier already had some information about the atomic weapon through his own intelligence sources and grasped the importance of Truman's words, or whether he took mention of a new weapon merely to mean a larger conventional bomb is not certain. Truman was deliberately casual in his comment to Stalin, and it was made without the help of an American interpreter. The President noted in his memoirs only that Stalin said he hoped the Americans would make good use of the new weapon against the Japanese.

The Americans learned at Potsdam, both from the Russians and from their own decoding of intercepted messages from Tokyo, that the Japanese had approached Moscow to mediate in the termination of the war. No terms were clearly specified, but the Japanese expressed a readiness to give up the territories occupied as a result of war. This information plus the existence of the atomic weapon still produced no serious reconsideration by the American Joint Chiefs of Staff of their effort to bring the Soviet Union into the war. They were still strongly of the opinion that the Red Army movement into China would relieve the United States of a major and costly military burden. Discussions of the strategy of this operation were held with Soviet military leaders at Potsdam. Stalin reported briefly to Truman on Russian talks with the Chiang Kai-shek government about the concessions in Manchuria that had been set at Yalta as compensation for the participation of the Soviet Union. Truman believed that he had convinced Stalin of the importance of maintaining an Open Door policy in Manchuria, but the President stood fully behind the Yalta arrangements.

A formal declaration to Japan was prepared at Potsdam and issued by the United States, Britain, and China. Unconditional surrender of the Japanese armed forces was called for, but the Japanese were assured that their sovereignty would be restored, and a peacetime economy with access to raw materials and world trade permitted. Some American experts on Japan urged that assurance be given that the Emperor would not be treated as a war criminal and would be permitted to retain his nominal position. They predicted this would increase Japanese readiness to surrender. Others favored a radical change in the Japanese political structure and opposed any pledge to retain the imperial framework. This difference of views was only resolved to the extent of deliberate ambiguity in the declaration's avoidance of any mention of the Emperor.

> We do not intend that the Japanese shall be enslaved as a race or destroyed as a nation, but stern justice shall be meted out to all war criminals, including those who have visited cruelties upon our prisoners. The Japanese government shall remove all obstacles to the revival and strengthening of democratic tendencies among the Japanese people. Freedom of speech, of religion and of thought, as well as respect for the fundamental human rights shall be established. . . . The occupying forces of the Allies shall be withdrawn from Japan as soon as these objectives have been accomplished and there has been established in accordance with the freely expressed will of the Japanese people a peacefully inclined and responsible government.

The Japanese were permitted to deduce whether or not this meant that Emperor Hirohito would be retained or punished as a war criminal.

The Cairo Declaration of 1943 was reaffirmed, stripping Japan of all territorial holdings beyond the home islands. Japan was not warned, however, of the new weapon and of its contemplated use. Some critics have believed such a warning might have produced a surrender before the Soviet Union entered the conflict. When the President was crossing the Atlantic on his sea voyage home, he was informed of what he called "the greatest thing in history," the incineration of a major portion of Hiroshima on August 6.

Truman returned to Washington with a protocol of twenty-one articles that expressed the "conclusions" of the Big Three's final meeting. Unlike Yalta, the only secret conclusions were those that involved Soviet entry into the war against Japan. Few of the twenty-one articles represented real agreements, clearly understood by all three parties. Those that did were reluctant compromises in which one or more signatories recognized that the *de facto* situation, while unfavorable to their interests, would be difficult and costly to change. The majority of the articles either deferred the issue to the consideration of the Council of Foreign Ministers or were loosely phrased statements that each power could interpret to serve its own interests.

With Eastern Europe and a large segment of Germany under the control of the Red Army, Stalin was able to return to Moscow, confident of his strength and hopeful that intransigent states like Turkey would recognize the need for concessions to a powerful neighbor. With the atomic bomb in American possession and a conviction that the Soviet Union was not likely to acquire equal power in the indefinite future, Truman was also able to return to his capital with confidence that matters deferred would be eventually settled favorably for the United States. Clement Attlee returned to a situation that made the struggle of his two giant allies a secondary matter. He was now Prime Minister of a small island, crowded and nearly bankrupt, with a mandate to create a Socialist Britain that would eradicate the major social and economic evils produced by more than a century of industrialization. In world affairs, Britain was to be clearly a junior partner of the United States, sometimes also a very restless and unhappy partner.

American hopes were fulfilled in one area, the settlement with Japan. Although the Soviet Union was given a post on the

eleven-power Far Eastern Advisory Commission that was pre-
sumed to guide the policy of the occupation forces, the United
States and the Supreme Commander of the Allied Powers, General
Douglas MacArthur, acted independently in matters of major importance. In agreeing to surrender, the Japanese asked that the Emperor be retained. The United States accepted that condition with
the qualification that the Emperor and his government were
subject to the authority of the Supreme Commander. Basic directives were written in Washington by the State-War-Navy Co-
ordinating Committee. The Far Eastern Commission had little
more influence than the Control Commissions established in Eastern Europe, where the Soviet Union carried out policies in its own
interests. The Commission was located in Washington, but an
Allied Council was established in Tokyo with Chinese, Russian,
British, and American representation. In this body both the Soviet
and British delegates often complained that they were ignored by
General MacArthur although they were to be consulted on major
substantive matters. The General's superiors in Washington had
similar complaints about being ignored, but the occupation program remained basically American in conception and implementation.

In preparing the Japanese peace treaty, the United States also
profited from its experience in Europe. The Truman administration
decided to avoid the impasses of the Council of Foreign Ministers,
where the Soviet Union could exercise the veto, and submit the
draft treaty to a two-thirds majority vote in the Far Eastern
Commission, where there was no provision for a veto. The Soviet
Union and the Chiang government of China both opposed such an
approach. The Chinese resented the leniency with which they
considered the Japanese were being treated by MacArthur.
There was some lingering Chinese resentment as well of the concessions made at Yalta to the Soviet Union at Chinese expense.
Washington decided that a peace treaty opposed by two major
belligerents created too many political problems, and the approach
through the Far Eastern Commission was withdrawn.

The outbreak of the Korean War in the summer of 1950

made a peace treaty with Japan seem essential even if it was likely to be rejected by the Soviet Union. The Japanese by this date had become an important asset in Asia with China transformed as a Communist state. American security considerations were now of primary importance in shaping the treaty. John Foster Dulles was given a special appointment by the State Department in September of 1950 as an experienced diplomat and major figure in the Republican Party. His task was to secure acceptance of an American draft treaty by a substantial number of nations through diplomatic channels. After Dulles began his work, a British draft was also prepared. The two drafts were combined in July of 1951 along with the revisions suggested by some of the states with whom Dulles conferred.

When enough agreement was assured, Washington called for a full-scale peace conference, but the invitations stated specifically that the meeting to be held in San Francisco in September of 1951 was "for conclusion and signature of a treaty with Japan on the terms of that text," the Anglo-American draft made public in August. Invitations were not limited to the eleven major belligerents on the Far Eastern Advisory Commission, but sent to fifty-five governments, including Japan and the United States. The British insisted that the major victim of Japanese expansion, China, be included, but Washington was unwilling to invite representatives of the new regime in Peking. Some states objected to inviting the Chiang Kai-shek regime on Formosa in the name of China, and by a compromise no Chinese government was invited. The other largest Asian power, India, rejected the invitation, unwilling to ratify a treaty that, by the terms of the draft, did not permit Japan to choose a neutral role in the Cold War. Article Six stated that nothing was to prevent the stationing of foreign troops in Japan under any bilateral agreements, a provision to allow for the continued use of Japanese soil by American forces.

The Soviet Union had protested the whole procedure followed by the United States and was not expected to attend the San Francisco meeting. When the American invitation was accepted, careful preparations were made to restrict the role of the Soviet delegation. Working with Britain as a co-sponsor of the conference, the United States set rules of procedure that limited the range of debate, barred treaty amendments from the agenda, and made no provision for great power veto. On this basis the treaty was signed without the Soviet Union succeeding in amending or changing the text. The Soviet representative refused to sign as did the delegates of Poland and Czechoslovakia. The same day the remaining delegates, forty-nine nations in all, signed the treaty, September 8, 1951, the United States also signed a bilateral Security Treaty with Japan. It provided for the retention of United States land, air, and sea forces in and about Japan. They were to be used for "the maintenance of international peace and security in the Far East," as well as being available on request of the Japanese government "to put down large-scale internal riots and disturbances in Japan, caused through instigation or intervention by an outside power or powers."

The Japanese Peace Treaty discarded the totally punitive outlook of Cairo, Yalta, and Potsdam. The reparations provision was a mild one, but Japan was required to renounce title to its former colonies, to the Kuriles and southern Sakhalin. The Treaty did not recognize Soviet possession of these areas. Claims to Formosa were renounced along with the islands of Micronesia, held under the League of Nations mandate. The United States was given the right to exercise jurisdiction over the strategically placed Ryukyu Islands, which had become an important American military base, but the Japanese were assured informally that they retained "residual sovereignty."

With China, India, Burma, and the Soviet Union refusing to sign the San Francisco treaty, the settlement of 1951 marked the end of any remnants of wartime unity in the Pacific. The Soviet Union did not regularize its relations with Japan until October of 1956, when a treaty was signed that left the territorial settlement to a *modus vivendi*. A Japanese peace treaty was signed with Nationalist China in 1952, but, while trade relations were re-established between Peking and Tokyo, no formal treaty was negotiated in the decade and a half following the San Francisco treaty.

In Europe in the same period of the fifties and sixties, no peace treaty was signed with a divided Germany. The West German *Bundesrepublik,* created out of the American, British, and French occupation zones, gradually acquired the marks of sovereignty, without being formally recognized by the Soviet Union. The East German Peoples Republic had its sovereignty recognized by the Communist world, but without recognition by London and Washington. The United States continued to refuse to recognize the *de facto* western boundaries of the Soviet Union, the boundaries of Poland, and the annexation of Lithuania, Latvia, and Estonia. These three former states continued to maintain legations in Washington and to be carried on the diplomatic lists of the Department of State. Official United States maps delineated their 1939 borders while noting that they were "administered" by the Soviet Union along with the northern part of East Prussia.

The map of Europe was the product, not so much of plan, but of spheres of influence created by spheres of power. The statements of aspirations, the exchanges of views, the written agreements played a minor part. Where the *de facto* situation was too unsatisfactory for the interests of a major power, it was refused legal recognition and the issue remained "unfinished business," underlying grievances of the Cold War.

10

How New the New World?

During the war years many minds outside of government circles turned to the problems of the future peace. Many plans were developed that promised a lasting period of warlessness. Private peace planners turned to the public for support, and from the presses came hundreds of books, pamphlets, and magazine articles outlining the desirable roads to the future. American and British citizens could choose from a great variety of blueprints the kind of society they believed desirable and possible, and organizations offered them a way of devoting their energies to their chosen ends.

Some writers took as their theme the title of the book of the 1940 Republican presidential candidate Wendell L. Willkie, *One World,* and advocated the abolition of the major prerogatives of national sovereignty. Their goal was the creation of a supranational state or world federation within which there would be no national armies capable of the conquest of neighboring states. Some, like Ely Culbertson, proposed eleven regional federations under a central world federation that would also have at its disposal an international army. Others, like Clarence Streit, whose *Union Now* attracted considerable attention in 1939, called for the federation of the United States and the British Commonwealth nations as the core of the future world order.

The one-world concept required radical socioeconomic changes according to Vice President Henry Wallace and many who thought along similar lines. In a speech made in May of 1942, Wallace proclaimed that the new century could and must be "the century of the Common Man." The war was to be part of a "long-drawn-out people's revolution" that would bring about a world-wide new democracy, synthesizing the best features of Anglo-American political democracy with the best features of the economic democracy proclaimed by the Soviet Union. In this world there would be a combination of "home rule and centralized authority."

Wallace and other one-worlders were dismissed as impractical visionaries by men who believed that the nation-state system should survive intact. What was required was a change of outlook by which national leaders realized that co-operation was really in their best interests and conflict a danger to all. Nations must be persuaded to live according to the aspirations of the Atlantic Charter, making generosity the rule of international life. A new international organization of sovereign states with American membership, and the League of Nations experience as a warning to induce co-operative behavior, would provide for peaceful coexistence.

There were Americans who called themselves internationalists who believed that it was unrealistic to place hope in a modernized version of the League. Petty squabbling would lead to serious conflicts if the peace was entrusted to the care of the collectivity of nations, large and small. Only the Big Four could really preserve the peace, having the power and responsibility combined. The smaller nations had to be taught to accept their status as the only realistic alternative to a world of insecurity and war.

Vigorous nationalists in all nations rejected the idea of a world run effectively by the Big Four in the interests of all. Speaking for a nation excluded by Roosevelt's plan, General de Gaulle attacked it as "a permanent system of intervention." The world had to return to the politics of power in which each state sought its own interests as wisely as possible. The most scholarly presentation of this point of view was that of Nicholas J. Spykman, who in 1942 shocked many planners with his book *America's Strategy in World Politics,* which argued in traditional terms for the restoration of a balance of power world. Spykman was farsighted enough to see that someday the United States would come to support Japan in Asia against a powerful China. To a nationalist like Henry Luce, the return to traditional world politics meant that the United States would replace Britain in its former role as a world leader. In a *Life* editorial in February of 1941, Luce said that this century, "if it is to come to life in any nobility of health and vigor, must be to a significant degree an American Century."

As the postwar decades have passed, none of the capsulated characterizations have proven apt in their description of the new age. It has belonged neither to the Common Man nor to the Americans. As for the One World, Winston Churchill finally advised the most belligerent Cold War advocates that while one world was still better than two, two worlds were still better than none. Only a term born in the closing days of the Pacific war had some descriptive validity, "the atomic age." It was the disintegration of the smallest particle of matter that brought something indisputably new to the postwar world.

From its birth, "the atomic age" was a term that carried connotations of hope and despair. The demolition of Hiroshima and Nagasaki finally brought some peace to large parts of the world, a peace greeted with joy by many. But there were also notes of gloom in August of 1945 over a new age that began in such a ruthless manner. The bomb may bring us victory quickly, wrote the *New York Times* military expert Hanson Baldwin, with the news of Hiroshima, but he predicted that it would "sow the seeds of hate more widely than ever." The American demonstration of power against living creatures "creates a bottomless wound in the living conscience of the race," was the judgment of *Time* magazine. Speaking for liberal Christianity, the *Christian Century* deplored that the greatest single effort ever made by human beings "ends only in a rapture of destruction which will henceforth overshadow all that remains to us of civilized feeling and the living spirit of man." Only when the tremendous possibilities of the peacetime use of atomic energy began to unfold was the term "atomic age" given a more optimistic connotation.

Man's venture into the depths of the skies created in the "space age" another claimant to characterize the newness of the postwar era. Like the exploration of the atom, the motivations that sent men and scientific equipment beyond the gravitational pull of the earth were closely associated with preparations for another war. All the sputniks could not escape their blood relationship to the German V-1 and V-2 rockets that blindly blasted the buildings and lives of Londoners in Hitler's last strike at Britain with his vengeance weapon. The United States and the Soviet Union competed with each other in the closing days of the European War in netting the Nazi scientists and data that would speed their own efforts to produce rocket weapons. Yet the movement into space also offered man a new hope, a perspective from which to see his little planet as one world, without the man-made lines that divided it and produced so many contests of destruction.

The newness contributed by the scientific developments contrasted strongly with the relative lack of change in the political world of nations where continuity demonstrated that the wartime governments were more capable of manipulating matter in new ways than of leading men to think along new lines politically. As in 1939, a dynamic and pervasive nationalism continued to be the world's strongest ideology. In the postwar decades it spread to the remotest global regions touched by colonialism. There it awakened men to new loyalties, larger than their old tribal or local loyalties, but still short of universal. By producing many additions to the prewar list of nations, nationalism seemed only to offer a greater variety of rivalries and alignments than did the old world. The quest for national power continued along traditional avenues.

Within the continuities there were changes for individual nations. Some gained power, some lost, processes which World War II in many instances only accelerated. The great empire of the Tsars revived at last after the setback of World War I and the ensuing civil wars. With the help of zealous leadership and the sacrifices of millions, Russia more than regained its 1914 boundaries with the major exception of Finland. The Eastern European states which lived in the 1930's in the shadow of Berlin found themselves coexisting in what Moscow would consider its aurora. The once-dominant Germany lived divided in defiance of the laws of nationalism. But both segments shared a concern for the *irredenta* of the Eastern lands, and the long wall that cut the former Reich in two could possibly be only a transient aberration. Britain and France, despite the title of victors, joined the ranks of lesser powers, occasionally denying and regretting the realities of their position. In Asia, Japan, restored to even greater economic power than in its imperialist days, found itself living alongside a China that no longer supinely invited conquest. Nearly a century late in following the Japanese example, China was rushing industrialization and making its claim to the status of major power that President Roosevelt had tried to confer on it prematurely.

This was a world far different from that hoped for by the visionary peace planners and far different from that which the Big Three had tried to create. It failed to fill many of the expectations of the three men who first met at Teheran.

Stalin had looked to the security of his people, twice invaded in twenty-five years, with a political technique that promised satisfactory results. A belt of Communist states in Eastern Europe was to mean "friendly governments," and an effective buffer to capitalist intrigues and armies. A Communist China whose possibilities were belatedly recognized by Moscow was to end the imperialist, capitalist era in Asia. A large part of the civilized world was thus to be secure and unified by a common ideology. But Communists also proved to be susceptible to the older pulls of nationalism. Within two decades the national interests of Communist states clashed with each other and with the Soviet Union. Communism did not seem likely to be the ideology that would join men as brothers despite the older political boundaries. A war between Communist states, as unthinkable to Lenin as a war between Christians would have been to the Apostles, was no longer an impossibility.

Roosevelt had looked to the security of the Four Policemen, expecting that the other three would defer to the leadership of the United States as the only nation that did not have to turn inward to restore its economy after the ravages of war. The President did not expect, as few did, the quick recovery of the Soviet Union and its determination to retain its wartime status in world affairs. Nor did Roosevelt see the extent to which financial strain and psychological weariness would press Britain into rapidly cutting its traditional commitments to Empire and to areas like Greece and Turkey. Roosevelt further refused to take seriously the warnings of China specialists that the Chiang Kai-shek regime was likely to crumble when the final confrontation took place with its so-called wartime allies, the Chinese Communist Party.

Roosevelt's final miscalculation was his failure to realize that his long battle with isolationism was more than won. Just before his death he still could not believe that American troops could possibly be kept in Europe for more than two years after victory. He did not foresee a world in which there would be a worldwide allocation of American forces along with interventions that produced frequent cries of "imperialism." The nation that in 1939 rejected Roosevelt's trial-balloon statement that its frontier was on the Rhine had evolved to the point where there were no frontiers that were not viewed as potentially essential elements in the security of the United States.

Despite his greater grasp of historical continuities than the other two leaders, Churchill also misjudged the immediate future. In his defense of Empire he failed to measure the intensity of the desire for independence on the part of "lesser breeds without the law." The Empire for which the Prime Minister fought was an empire already in large part alienated and willing to shed blood for its own independence. Not only India, but Africa and even the West Indies and British Guiana were no longer willing to live under the political guidance of London. The people of Britain, at the same time, were unwilling to pay the price necessary if the Empire were to be retained by force.

The miscalculations of the Big Three is no proof that they were inferior in vision and wisdom to their peace-making pre-decessors at Westphalia and after. The planners of the seventeenth century had similar problems, as George Clark has pointed out in *War and Society in the Seventeenth Century:*

> The enemy narrowed down the field of the possible; allies exacted concessions that were incompatible with the original purposes, and neutrals took advantage of their opportunities. The statesmen themselves found their policy superseded, perhaps by something more modest, perhaps by something more ambitious, always by something new. War created policy rather than continued.

The problems of coalitions are not new. Produced by fear of a common enemy, wartime unity has frequently turned to hostility and even warfare when that enemy is no longer dangerous. "A drowning man grasps at a serpent," said a nineteenth-century Ottoman sultan, defending his alliance with his ancient Russian enemy in the face of an Egyptian invader. But when the drowning man succeeds in being rescued, he chooses his associates with care and may even join a crusade against serpents.

The great change from the world of 1939 was that the nations of the postwar world faced a common enemy in war itself. The destructive capacity of man had outrun rational limits. The feats of devastation achieved in World War II began to shrink in significance compared to the postwar potentials. The B-29 Super-Fortress was able to travel thousands of miles and unload enough destructive power to eliminate an entire city block and all of its inhabitants. In March of 1943 a record was established when more than three hundred of these bombers gutted the city of Tokyo and killed approximately a hundred thousand people in one air raid. But within twenty years a larger bomber, the B-52, with a nuclear weapon, was capable of delivering a blow equal to a fleet of five million B-29's with their conventional bombs. One plane thus carried the potential for wiping out five million city blocks and their inhabitants. The total land- and sea-based missiles of the United States and Soviet Union had a destructive capacity capable of eliminating civilized society on the entire globe.

The new enemy, poisoning the air and soil over great areas, was a threat to belligerent and neutral. The most powerful nuclear nation had no effective defense against its greatest rival, and could only insure that the people of an aggressor nation would die as quickly. The atomic dusts, whirling about the globe, would be impartial in their disregard for political boundaries in depositing their fatal radioactivity. Nations did have a powerful reason to unite for their common defense, which did not exist in 1939. This was a new world. Existence of all states required acceptance of coexistence and measures to prevent the nuclear enemy from escaping the rational control of man.

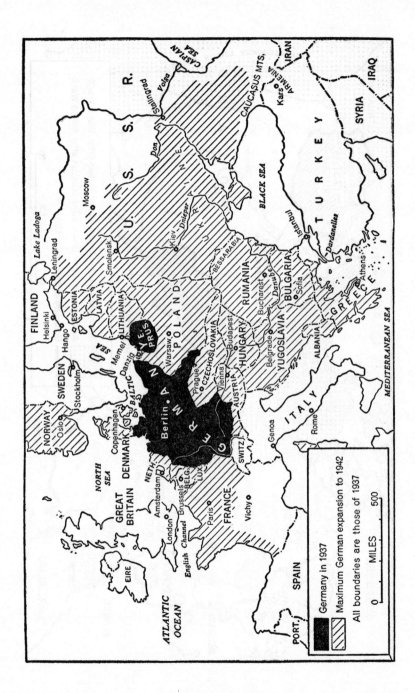

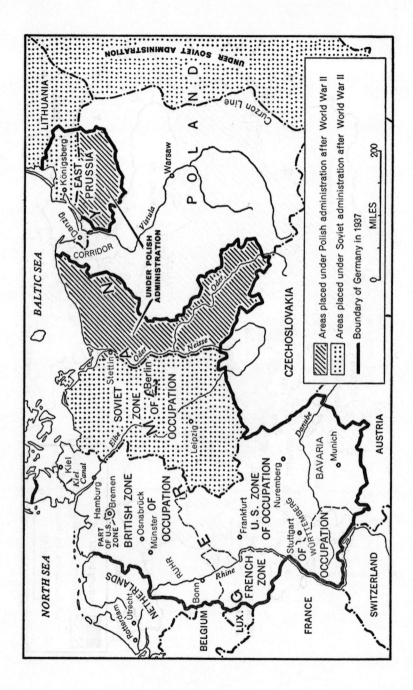

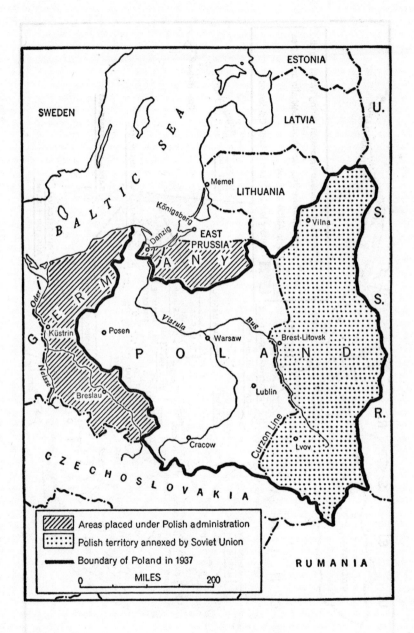

SWEDEN

BALTIC SEA

ESTONIA

LATVIA

Memel

LITHUANIA

Königsberg

Danzig

EAST
PRUSSIA

GERMANY

Vilna

U.

S.

S.

Odder

Küstrin

Posen

Visrula

Warsaw

Bug

Brest-Litovsk

N

POLAND

D

Neisse

Breslau

Lublin

Curzon Line

R.

Cracow

Lvov

CZECHOSLOVAKIA

Areas placed under Polish administration

Polish territory annexed by Soviet Union

Boundary of Poland in 1937

MILES
0   200

RUMANIA

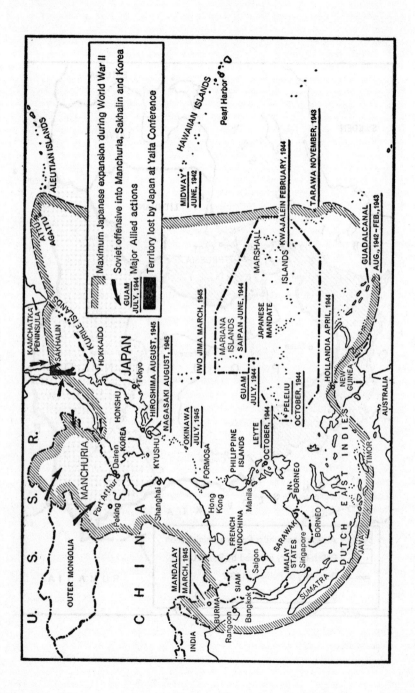

Bibliographical Essay

1. THE PERSISTENT TASK

The process of peace-making in the last three or four centuries has not been treated comprehensively either as a narrative or analytically. A British diplomat and scholar Ernest Satow, in the first edition of his *Guide to Diplomatic Practice* (2 vols., London, 1917), compiled a list of the major peace conferences since 1648, but only summarized each briefly. The peace conferences are also dealt with briefly in the major surveys of diplomatic history such as David J. Hill's *A History of Diplomacy in the International Development of Europe* (3 vols., London, 1905–14) and in the Russian survey edited by V. Potiemkine, *Histoire de la diplomatie* (3 vols., Paris, 1946), subsequently revised in the Russian edition. The best modern guide to the peace conferences, as well as to the diplomacy that preceded them, is the French series *Histoire des relations internationales,* edited by Pierre Renouvin (7 vols., 1953–57). Some useful historical materials are gathered in the work of a British jurist, Coleman Philipson, *Termination of War and Treaties of Peace* (New York, 1916).

The literature on specific peace conferences is too extensive to be dealt with here, but a few outstanding works deserve mention, such as C. V. Wedgwood's *The Thirty Years War* (London, 1938) for its treatment of the Peace of Westphalia. Harold Nicolson's *The Congress of Vienna* (New York, 1946), was written by a historian-diplomat who looked backward from the personal experiences that produced his *Peacemaking, 1919* (New York, 1933).

2. NATIONAL TRADITIONS AND AMBITIONS

The voluminousness of the literature on Versailles and the period between the two world wars makes any brief bibliography highly selective. The books cited here were of particular value to me because of a point of view, stimulating hypotheses, or the high quality of the narrative.

Two brief volumes, both written before the flood of memoirs and the opening of the official archives, are still fine introductions to this period. The first is the work of a versatile British scholar, E. H. Carr, whose *International Relations Between the Two World Wars, 1919–1939* (London, 1947) remains a fine work of synthesis. The other is Arnold Wolfer's *Britain and France Between Two Wars* (New York, 1940), outdated in many respects, but of continuing value.

In addition to the many earlier studies of various aspects of Versailles, Arno J. Mayer's *Political Origins of the New Diplomacy, 1917–1918* (New Haven, 1959) is now essential in emphasizing the impact of the "leftist-internationalist" line of thought on the peace, with its reinforcement in Lenin's pronouncements. W. W. Gottlieb's *Studies in Secret Diplomacy During the First World War* (London, 1957) points up the basic outlook of the Allied Powers in dealing with the intervention of Turkey and Italy.

For British foreign policy in this period a good introductory volume is P. A. Raynold's *British Foreign Policy in the Inter-War Years.* Martin Gilbert and Richard Gott's *The Appeasers* (Boston, 1963) is a lively and controversial volume that treats the period from 1933 to the outbreak of the war. Equally lively and controversial are the relevant chapters in A. J. P. Taylor's *English History, 1914–1945* (London, 1965).

Keith Feiling's *Neville Chamberlain* (London, 1946) is a sympathetic biography of the heavily criticized Prime Minister. Lord Templewood's (Sir Samuel Hoare) *Nine Troubled Years* (London, 1954) is an even stronger defense of appeasement. *Failure of a Mission* by Sir Nevile Henderson is the account of the last British Ambassador to Berlin.

French foreign policy in the intrawar years is treated with special attention by the general diplomatic histories of that country's leading historians of foreign relations. Pierre Renouvin's *Les relations internationales, 1914–1945* (Paris, 1948) and J. B. Duroselle's *Histoire diplomatique de 1919 à nos jours* (Paris, 1953) are both useful surveys. A more recent work of greater concentration is René Albrecht-Carrié's *France, Europe and the Two World Wars* (Geneva, 1960). The defeatist outlook of France in 1939 and 1940 is described in the personal testimony of Marc Bloch in *Strange Defeat* (London, 1949). The Maginot strategy is described by Vivian Rowe in *The Great Wall of France* (London, 1959).

The first year of the warless war in the West is described from the British point of view by E. S. Turner in *The Phoney War* (New York, 1961) and by Laurence Thompson in *1940, Year of Legend* (London, 1966). The military-political planning is covered in the official history by J. R. M. Butler, editor, *Grand Strategy* (6 vols., London, 1956–   ), Vol. II, for the period September 1939 to June 1941.

A good, brief survey of German foreign policy is provided by Lionel Kochan's *Struggle for Germany, 1914–1945* (Edinburgh, 1963). Hans Gatzke's *Germany's Drive to the West* (Baltimore, 1950) is a study of one aspect of German policy during World War I that throws light on later ambitions. Any evaluation of Hitler's role calls for reading A. J. P. Taylor's *The Origins of the Second World War* (New York, 1961), along with the counterarguments of its critics. Hugh Trevor-Roper's attack on Taylor along with other dissenting views is reprinted in *The Outbreak of the Second World War: Design or Blunder?*, edited by John L. Snell (Boston, 1962).

Hitler's views on German foreign policy are to be found in Alan Bullock's *Hitler: A Study in Tyranny* (New York, 1952) and in *Hitler's Secret Conversations, 1941–1944*, edited by H. Trevor-Roper (New York, 1953). How the *Führer* tried to apply these ideas in wartime is surveyed by *Hitler's Europe*, edited by Arnold and Veronica Toynbee (New York, 1954) and by Gerald Reitlinger's *The House Built on Sand: The Conflict of German Policy in Russia, 1939–1945* (New York, 1960).

Italian foreign policy is covered in Ivone Kirkpatrick's biography *Mussolini* (New York, 1964), and in some special detail in Elizabeth Wiskemann's *The Rome-Berlin Axis* (New York, 1949). It is defended by Luigi Villari's *Italian Foreign Policy Under Mussolini* (New York, 1956).

The role of continuity in Russian foreign policy is a matter of much dispute. One of the best efforts at coping with it is the symposium *Russian Foreign Policy: Essays in Historical Perspective*, edited by Ivo J. Lederer (New Haven, 1962). E. H. Carr deals with the subject in a thoughtful essay "The Legacy of History" in the first volume of his *Socialism in One Country* (3 vols., New York, 1958–64). Max Beloff's *The Foreign Policy of Soviet Russia, 1929–1941* (2 vols., New York, 1947–49), is a good pioneering work.

The special area emphasis of the title adds to the value of John A. Lukacs' *The Great Powers and Eastern Europe* (New York, 1953), covering the period between the wars in some detail. The short background essays of *The World in March 1939*, edited by Arnold Toynbee and Frank Ashton-Gwatkin (New York, 1952), make it an exceptionally good survey of the policies of the leading European and Asian powers.

3. PEACE AS AN AMERICAN INTEREST

The establishment of the Inquiry and some of its early statements are printed in *Foreign Relations of the United States, 1919, Paris Peace Conference* (13 vols., Washington, D.C., 1942–47), Volume 1. The organization is analyzed by Lawrence E. Gelfand's *The Inquiry: American Preparations for Peace, 1917–1919* (New Haven, 1963). David F. Trask's *The United States in the Supreme War Council: American War Aims and Inter-Allied Strategy, 1917–1918* (Middletown, Conn., 1965), presents another side of the preliminary decision-making.

Sumner Welles gives a full account of his mission in *The Time For Decision* (New York, 1944). Additional details are to be found in *Foreign Relations of the United States, 1940*, Vol. 1.

Winston Churchill gives a British report on the Atlantic Conference in *The Grand Alliance* (Boston, 1950), with additional details in the third volume of the Grand Strategy series (London, 1964). Robert Sherwood's *Roosevelt and Hopkins* (New York, 1948) was the first detailed American version of the writing of the Charter. A full account of the discussions is to be found in William L. Langer and S. Everett Gleason's *The Undeclared War, 1940–41* (New York, 1953), Chapter XXI.

4. ROOSEVELT: THE PERSONAL EQUATION

Franklin Roosevelt is still too controversial a figure in recent American history to be the subject of thorough and well-balanced biographical studies. His two major biographers Frank Freidel and Arthur Schlesinger Jr. have some years to cover before evaluating his wartime career. The best biography that covers the war years is James MacGregor Burns's *Roosevelt: The Lion and the Fox* (New York, 1956). In addition to the views of his foreign policy decisions offered by the Hopkins papers, the books of two Cabinet members are of considerable value. The second volume of *The Memoirs of Cordell Hull* (New York, 1948) covers the areas of foreign policy in which the Secretary of State was allowed to participate, while *On Active Service in Peace and War* by Henry L. Stimson and McGeorge Bundy (New York, 1948) offers the more critical views of the Secretary of War. The forthcoming third volume of the Morgenthau diary, edited by John Blum, will be another major contribution with Roosevelt's foreign policy seen from the Treasury Department by its Secretary and close associate of the President. For American policy this chapter has also relied on the *Foreign Relations* volumes for 1941 and 1942.

Churchill's memoirs have been supplemented by his Foreign Minister's *The Eden Memoirs: The Reckoning* (London, 1965), covering the war years. The Foreign Office role is also narrated in the official history of Llewellyn Woodward, *British Foreign Policy in the Second World War* (London, 1962), based on the archival materials.

5. THE MILITARY PERIMETERS OF THE PEACE

Any discussion of the politico-military strategy of World War II must rely directly or indirectly to some extent on the British Grand Strategy series, cited above, and the official United States Army series. The particularly relevant volumes in the latter series are Mark S. Watson's *Chief of Staff: Prewar Plans and Preparations* (Washington, 1950), Ray S. Cline's *Washington Command Post: The Operations Division* (Washington, 1951), and *Strategic Planning for Coalition Warfare, 1941–1942* by Maurice Matloff and Edwin Snell (Washington, 1953). This Army team of historians has also produced a valuable collection of short essays *Command Decisions*, published commercially, under the editorship of Kent R. Greenfield (New York, 1959). The original publication of these essays by the Government Printing Office also includes Maurice Matloff's "The 90 Division Gamble," a valuable discussion of American manpower limitations.

Three relatively short volumes discuss the general strategy of the war from the American and British point of view: Kent R. Greenfield's *American Strategy in World War II: A Reconsideration* (Baltimore, 1963), Samuel E. Morison's *Strategy and Compromise* (Boston, 1958), and *The Second World War*, the work of that irascible British military historian Major-General J. F. C. Fuller (London, 1948). One specialized study is particularly relevant, Trumbull Higgins' *Winston Churchill and the Second Front, 1940–1943* (New York, 1957).

The debate over the strategic bombing program has been largely conducted in Britain with no major challenges of the Air Force coming from the United States. C. P. Snow's *Science and Government* (Cambridge, Mass., 1961) launched the attack and extended it in his *A Postscript to Science and Government* (Cambridge, Mass., 1962). In the latter lectures Snow drew on the findings of the official British history *The Strategic Air Offensive Against Germany, 1939–1945*, written by Charles Webster and Noble Frankland (4 vols., London, 1961). The findings are also discussed by Noble Frankland in his *The Bombing Offensive Against Germany* (London, 1965). A particularly brutal bombing venture is described by David Irving's *The Destruction of Dresden* (New York, 1964). Churchill's advisor Lindeman is defended by his biographer the Earl of Birkenhead in *The Professor and the Prime Minister: The Official Life of Viscount Cherwell* (Boston, 1962).

Supplementing the Churchill view of war strategy is the most important of the British memoirs, compiled by Sir Arthur Bryant, *The Turn of the Tide* (London, 1957) and *Triumph in the West* (London, 1959), from the diaries of Lord Alanbrooke. Roosevelt's role as a strategist is discussed by William Emerson, "Franklin Roosevelt as Commander-in-Chief," *Military Affairs*, XXII (Winter 1958–59), 181–207.

6. A STRAINED AND STRANGE ALLIANCE

Two Moscow observers of Russo-American relations have written memoirs: John R. Deane in *The Strange Alliance* (New York, 1947), and William H. Standley with the assistance of Arthur A. Ageton in *Admiral Ambassador to Russia* (Chicago, 1955). Something of the Russian point of view is presented by Alexander Werth in *Russia at War, 1941–1945* (New York, 1964). One Soviet volume has been translated, G. Deborin's *The Second World War* (Moscow, n.d.), unfortunately relying heavily on Western writings seen through Soviet eyes. The range of Soviet biases are covered by Matthew P. Gallagher's *The Soviet History of World War II: Myths, Memories and Realities,* and viewed in turn with strong American biases (New York, 1963).

Some of the ambivalence in American thought is described by Raymond Dawson in *The Decision to Aid Russia, 1941* (Chapel Hill, 1959). Andrew J. Schwartz's *America and the Russo-Finnish War* (Washington, 1960) touches on the effects of that event. Warren B. Walsh in "American Attitudes Toward Russia," *Antioch Review,* VII (Summer, 1947), 183–190, and Paul Willen's "Who 'Collaborated' With Russia?" *Antioch Review,* XIV (Fall, 1954), 259–283, survey American opinion in wartime.

The Polish issue is presented by an ardent exponent, the Ambassador to Washington, Jan Ciechanowski, in *Defeat In Victory* (New York, 1947), and by Edward J. Rozek in *Allied Wartime Diplomacy: A Pattern in Poland* (New York, 1958). A more critical evaluation of the Polish position is offered by Samuel L. Sharp in *Poland: White Eagle on a Red Field* (Cambridge, Mass., 1953). A plea for the present *de facto* Oder-Neisse boundary is made by B. Wiewiora in *The Polish-*

German Frontier in the Light of International Law (Poznan, 1964), while a call for the restoration of the lost German territories is presented by Friedrich von Wilpert's *The Oder-Neisse Problem* (New York, 1964).

7 and 8. QUEBEC, MOSCOW, AND TEHERAN: 1943; POLAND, GERMANY, AND YALTA: 1944–45

The most detailed histories of wartime diplomacy are Herbert Feis's *Churchill, Roosevelt, Stalin* (Princeton, 1957), written with access to State Department files and by an "insider" with a long State Department career and strongly nationalist point of view; and William H. McNeill's *America, Britain and Russia: Their Co-operation and Conflict, 1941–1946* (New York, 1953). The latter volume is the work of an American scholar but written for the Royal Institute of International Affairs in their valuable survey series edited by Arnold Toynbee. Although a number of source collections have become available since these two volumes were written, all subsequent writers will be indebted to these pioneering ventures into this deepening maze of materials. Two brief paperback surveys are John L. Snell's *Illusion and Necessity: The Diplomacy of Global War, 1939–1945* (Boston, 1963) and Gaddis Smith's *American Diplomacy During the Second World War, 1941–1945* (New York, 1965), both careful works of synthesis and making the conventional American indictment of Stalin and Soviet foreign policy.

The *Foreign Relations* Series compiled by the Department of State has issued the basic documents and background materials for the major conferences down to Potsdam with the annual volumes, now reaching 1944, providing documents and exchanges on issues that the Big Three did not cover. British records remain closed for the war period. A voluminous Roosevelt-Churchill correspondence exists in the Roosevelt Hyde Park Library, released by the British Foreign Office, but closed to me and presumably other historians by the State Department and the Department of Defense. A Russian contribution has been the publication of the correspondence of Churchill and Roosevelt with Stalin, including materials still classified in London and Washington: *Correspondence Between the Chairman of the Council of Ministers of the U.S.S.R. and the Presidents of the U.S.A. and the Prime Minister of Great Britain During the Great Patriotic War of 1941–1945* (2 vols., Moscow, 1957). The Soviet Union has also published in its monthly *International Affairs,* beginning in 1961, its transcriptions of the conferences of the war leaders at Teheran, Yalta, and Potsdam. For the most part these transcriptions are skimpy, compared to the American records, and usually of more interest for what they omit than what they add to the existing documentation.

Some special studies deserve mention. Herbert Feis has tackled the still politically sensitive China story in his *The China Tangle* (Princeton, 1953). His account has now been ably supplemented by Tang Tsou in *America's Failure in China, 1941–1950* (Chicago, 1963). Another viewpoint, but not a balanced one, is offered by Theodore White's *The Stilwell Papers* (New York, 1948). General Joseph W. Stilwell's strong criticism of Chiang is countered with possibly greater bias by his successor General Albert C. Wedemeyer in *Wedemeyer Reports* (New York, 1958).

The Yalta Conference was treated by the new Secretary of State Edward R. Stettinius Jr. in *Roosevelt and the Russians,* edited by Walter Johnson (Garden City, 1949). A good series of essays on various aspects of Yalta has been collected by John L. Snell as editor in *The Meaning of Yalta* (Baton Rouge, La., 1956).

9. POTSDAM AND THE COLD WAR MOOD

Along with the studies and memoirs listed above, the Potsdam Conference story is told by President Truman in his *Memoirs, Year of Decisions* (Garden City, 1955). James Byrnes, who was at Yalta, played a more important role at Potsdam and has recorded his memories in *Speaking Frankly* (New York, 1947) and *All In One Lifetime* (New York, 1958).

Herbert Feis devoted a volume to Potsdam alone, *Between War and Peace* (Princeton, 1960), using the records published by the State Department that same year. A very critical treatment of Potsdam and Truman's early diplomatic ventures is Gar Alperovitz' *Atomic Diplomacy: Hiroshima and Potsdam* (New York, 1965) which sees the prospect of the bomb as an important factor in hardening the American Cold War position.

Dumbarton Oaks, the San Francisco Conference, and the background planning for the United Nations are all treated in detail in Ruth B. Russell's *A History of the United Nations Charter: The Role of the United States, 1940–1945* (Washington, 1958).

Two articles on the German settlement by Philip E. Mosely deserve special mention, "Dismemberment of Germany," in *Foreign Affairs,* Vol. 28 (April, 1950), 487–98, and "The Occupation of Germany," in the same journal, Vol. 28 (July, 1950), 580–604.

10. HOW NEW THE NEW WORLD?

Most studies of the future peace written during the war years appear curiously irrelevant due to their optimism about the radical rearrangements that were to take place in the character of the international system. Of importance are Walter Lippmann's *U.S. War Aims* (Boston, 1944), and the earlier study of the same writer, *U.S. Foreign Policy: Shield of the Republic* (Boston, 1943). Widely read was E. H. Carr's *Conditions of Peace* (New York, 1942), which assumed the creation of an international order.

Clarence Streit published his *Union Now* in 1939 (New York) and *Union Now With Britain* in 1941 (New York). An early survey of the many ideas being framed is Arthur C. Millspaugh's *Peace Plans and American Choices* (Washington, 1942). Theodore Paullin published a brief survey *Comparative Peace Plans* (Philadelphia, 1943), which also analyzed some of the proposals. The writings of Wendell L. Willkie, Herbert Hoover, Henry Wallace, and Sumner Welles are collected in *Prefaces to Peace: A Symposium* (New York, 1944).

Index

Concessions, limited power to make, 3; to the Soviet Union, 63–65
Conservative Party, British, 169
Constantinople, 25, 26
Control Commission, 105
Corsica, 24
Council of Foreign Ministers, 169–70, 174, 177, 178
Crimean War, 75
Cross, Samuel, 67
Crowe, Sir Eyre, 15
Culbertson, Ely, 182
Curzon line, 58, 98, 108, 118, 119, 128, 145, 146
Czechoslovakia, 18, 19, 23, 27, 58, 84, 173, 180

D-Day, 83, 85
Daily Worker, 91
Dairen, Manchuria, 122, 153, 154
Daladier Édouard, 41–42
Daniels, Jonathan, 164
Davies, Joseph, 91, 165
Dean, Maj. General John, 88
Declaration of the United Nations, 50, 61–62, 68
Declaration on General Security (1943), 113, 124
Declaration on Liberated Europe, 150, 151, 161
Declaration Regarding Italy (1943), 110, 111, 112
Declining empires, 11
de Gaulle, General Charles, 61, 102, 105, 106, 121, 131, 140, 141, 147, 183
De jure belli et pacis (Grotius), 5
Denmark, 23, 43, 108
Destroyers for military bases agreement, 77
Disarmament, desirability for, 40
Dulles, John Foster, 179
Dumbarton Oaks Conference (1944), 154–56, 167
Dunkerque, British flight at, 73
Dutch East Indies, 69, 102

Eastern Front, 75, 85, 86, 162
East German People's Republic, 181
East Prussia, 100, 119, 126, 128, 173, 181

Eden, Anthony, 19, 51, 53, 57, 58–59, 63–64, 65, 66, 69, 93, 95, 96–97, 100, 101, 102, 103, 104, 105, 107, 112, 114, 121, 122, 128, 136, 140, 143, 148, 152, 153, 157, 168, 169
Egypt, 158
Eighth Air Force, U.S., 82
Eisenhower, General Dwight D., 80, 84–85, 110, 115, 133, 165, 168
Estonia, 18, 29, 58, 97, 181
Ethical considerations of peacemaking, 4–5
Ethiopia, 24, 27, 157, 158
European Advisory Commission, 112–14, 120, 131

Far East, 123, 154
Far East Advisory Commission, 178, 179
Finland, 24, 26, 29, 40, 42, 58, 97, 126, 170
Foreign Ministers' Conference, *see* Moscow Foreign Ministers' Conference
Formosa, 29, 179, 180
Forster, E. M., 2
Fortune magazine, 91
Four Freedoms, 43–44, 49, 50
Fourteen Points, 35, 36–37, 38, 48
France, 59, 68, 105, 169; Britain's attitude toward, 102; expansionist goals of, 143; fall of, 73, 77; imperialism, end of, 102, 121; military losses in World War II, 85; military strategy of, 72, 73; national growth of, 12–13; national traditions and ambitions, 16–18; on Reparations Committee, 166; restoration of, 121, 138; share in Germany occupation program, 140–41; *see also* Free French
Franco, General Francisco, 122
Franco-Soviet Pact (1935), 17
Frankland, Noble, 82
Free French, 61, 102, 105–06, 121
French Army, 72
French Indo-China, 69, 121

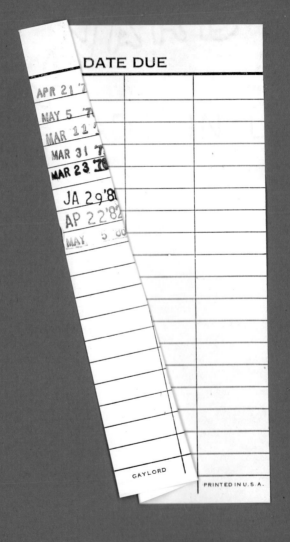

DATE DUE

APR 21 '7
MAY 5 '7
MAR 11 '
MAR 31 '7
MAR 23 '78
JA 29'80
AP 22'82
MAY 5 '86